Hamptons Modern

Hamptons Modern

**Contemporary Living
on the East End**

David Sokol

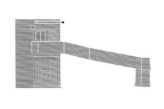

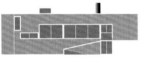

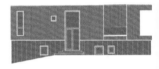
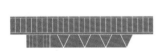

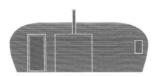
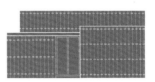

It Comes in Waves

"Proceed to highlighted route. Proceed to highlighted route," my phone beseeches with increasing urgency, and perhaps a touch of disdain. It is a balmy morning in September 2021, and a noon appointment at the home designed by Hal Goldstein for Scott Frances and Patti Weinberg (page 84) is fast approaching. Yet, as I drive from Sag Harbor's whaling-port center to an outlying part of this village on Long Island's South Fork, preservation-minded homes give way to modernistic flights that demand a closer look. In my journey's final quarter mile alone, there are three intriguing residences under construction for which curiosity-driven detours take priority over AI-generated pleas.

Outside of California, no place in America has been as synonymous with progressive residential architecture as the twin forks that make up Long Island's East End. Communities like New Canaan, Connecticut, Maine's Mount Desert Island, and Sarasota, Florida, experienced legendary, albeit finite, periods of architectural risk-taking in the mid-twentieth century. In other regions like Bucks County, Pennsylvania, and the suburbs of Northern Virginia, contemporary designs have just now begun to cast historic and tradition-oriented neighborhoods in exciting relief. Still others that have been sprinkled with experimental buildings over a long span, such as New York's Hudson Valley, are only recently witnessing that energy coalesce into an identifiable legacy (the primary assertion of my 2018 book, *Hudson Modern*).

The East End beats all these locations in terms of continuity and ambition. Modernism may not dominate the region's housing vocabulary, especially during times of economic anxiety. But since 1939, when developer Richard B. Allen asked architect Alfred Scheffer to help rebuild Amagansett's Beach Hampton subdivision from the Great New England Hurricane of the previous year, the region has repeatedly offered itself as a test bed for new building. Philip Johnson and Pierre Chareau completed milestone houses in 1940s-era Sagaponack and East Hampton, respectively. The following decade opened on the model home in Quogue that George Nelson and Gordon Chadwick had designed for *Holiday* magazine, as well as modernism's spread to the North Fork with Tony Smith's 1951 house in East Marion for the painter Theodoros Stamos. Within short order, the East End sprouted with additional important projects, as well as whole bodies of work by architects like Peter Blake, Barbara and Julian Neski, and Charles Gwathmey.

These and subsequent efforts at adapting and democratizing modernism have shaped the vocabulary of architecture worldwide. Closer to home, they presaged my distraction-laden journey through Sag Harbor: the East End's groundbreaking designs have made it easier for homeowners and professional designers to embrace modernism today. While this book is named after the cluster of communities most strongly associated with adventurous building, *Hamptons Modern* features houses on both forks (and as far west as Bellport, which has become a cultural gateway to the Hamptons) to evidence the phenomenon.

Like my previous exploration of the Hudson Valley, *Hamptons Modern* surveys eighteen recently completed residential projects. Both books also include three interviews that place local expression in broader context. Yet the books' goals differ, thanks to the very commonness of contemporary design on Long Island's East End.

Relying on a relatively limited number of homes, *Hudson Modern* argued that a never-before-seen critical mass of architects had tailored modernist ideals to the landscape, climate, and mindset of the Hudson Valley. On the other hand, the East End has amassed a plethora of masterful compositions and three-dimensional polemics over eighty-some-odd years. Meanwhile, writers and historians have repeatedly established this region's modernist bona fides, with incisive critique and expansive research. The point of *Hamptons Modern*, then, is not so much to observe a movement for the first time but to broadcast the best attributes of its current wave.

Indeed, the residences most recently completed on the East End do not resemble the modern houses realized at similar watershed moments forty or even fifteen years ago. In the 1970s, "environmental performance" was code for an ungainly building wielding clumsy new technology or requiring its occupants to orchestrate a series of moving parts according to weather conditions. And when Houses at Sagaponac developer Harry "Coco" Brown passed away in 2005, Apple had not yet released the first iPhone. In 2022, sustainability is both expected and elegant, and everything from taxi rides to short-term renters are within a keystroke's reach. Buildings embody these shifts, just as the East End buildings completed five years from now will likely be influenced by the COVID-19 pandemic and the battle over accessory dwelling units unfolding in states across America.

While East End modernism differs between eras, its current examples do not read from the same script. Some were developed speculatively, while others were conceived as family heirlooms; some wear modernism like an aesthetic, others are strongly informed by its values; some trumpet occupants' status while others do not aim to please the neigh-bors or stoke their envy. Some deflect public view altogether.

The residences spotlighted in *Hamptons Modern* all fall into the latter categories—the forever homes, the principled designs, and the unselfconscious acts. If there was one criterion by which this book's projects and interviewees alike were selected, it would be a deep feeling for Long Island's modernist heritage.

Hamptons Modern is divided into three parts, as a way of organizing the East End's abundance into unifying themes. In "Stewarding the Past" the affinity for local precedent is most palpable. This section focuses largely on careful modernizations of houses designed by some of the area's more prolific architects around the time of Nelson and Gwathmey. Not unlike vintage garments or furniture designs, which pass in and out of style, architectural objects are also subject to the changing tides of trend. The projects in "Stewarding" suggest late modernism's return to favor, as well as increasing popular understanding of reuse as an environmentally responsible act. Commissions by Young Projects and Ted Porter Architecture, which interact with and reflect upon nineteenth- and early-twentieth-century construction (pages 38 and 60), are also woven into the section. Among other points, this pair of entries underscores how East End modernism has been practiced with sensitivity to local landscape and deep-seated material culture since its inception.

The residences chosen for "Extending the Legacy" do not feature physical remnants of the past as found in previous chapters. Although these buildings were erected on greenfield sites or occupy the footprints of a previous structure that had been neglected, they too engage in dialogue with historic modernism.

As Goldstein told me the afternoon of my visit to Sag Harbor last September, his design of Redwood Residence draws from the first instances of coastal modernism on the Eastern Seaboard. Of course, neither Goldstein nor his peers would merely cut and paste modernism from the first half of the twentieth century. The architects featured in *Hamptons Modern* regard their practices as long-term undertakings—they are fulfilling a personally held concept of the built environment as much as they are providing services to clients—and in these homes, they exercise their vision. They must also dovetail projects with circumstances that their predecessors did not encounter. Who of the circa-1970 crowd could have foreseen that East End housing would become so large, close together, and capital-intensive as a matter of kind?

Caveats aside, "Extending" brims with references to the historical continuum. One might detect the Neskis' influence in the confident treatment of solid and void in the Desai Chia–designed Montauk House (page 104) or Blake's stacked volumes in the Shore House completed by Leroy Street Studio for a site in North Haven (page 136). There are respective hints of Myron Goldfinger's Anthony and Nina Petrocelli House and of the Ward Bennett–designed Sugarman House in the projects by toshihiro oki architect and Christoff:Finio shown on pages 94 and 148. All four of these examples also arguably owe a debt to the midcentury works of Harry Bates, who is one half of Bates Masi + Architects, featured in this book's final third.

This final section, entitled "Setting New Precedents," actively speculates on how the continuum will stretch into the future. If the residences in "Extending" reconcile the geometries, materials, and spirit of modernism with present-day conditions, then those chosen for "Setting" imagine forces like densification and climate change, which will dominate conversations about the North and South Forks in the coming decades. In the center of Amagansett, Bates's partner Paul Masi occupies a home where his family simultaneously enjoys downtown life and rural quiet, while the Ryall Sheridan Architects–designed Wetlands House gives form to the sea levels and storm surges that increasingly affect the coastline (pages 210 and 186). In addition to addressing these emerging problems, the section shows where East End architecture's long-standing reputation for formal and technological experimentation may head next, in projects like Springs House by Michael Haverland (page 166).

Realizing *Hamptons Modern* involved many tasks prior to writing, and selecting houses and interviewees for inclusion may have been the most time-consuming. Over that yearslong process, I paid keener attention than usual to portrayals of the East End: it's dead, and then it's back; it represents everything detestable about late capitalism one day and the promise of American meritocracy the next; it's a circus, or a haven. The media drumbeat is steady and manic. I chose this material to honor landscape, celebrate design excellence, and meditate on the meaning of home, rather than support one of those flashier narratives. But I acknowledge that commentators could very well bootstrap any of the stories that follow to suit their perceptions of Long Island's ribbonlike end. Architecture is never just about architecture, after all. I look forward to those interpretations as well as your own conclusions.

Stewarding the Past

Q&A with Timothy Godbold

It's no surprise that a book like *Hamptons Modern* should come from a child of suburban Long Island. The North and South Fork farms that had been field trip destinations morphed and dwindled before my eyes. Battles over the size or placement of new Hamptons homes were retold in the newspapers, and the architectural feats of these beach houses wended their ways into renovations taking place along my hometown's streets and cul-de-sacs. Putting together a book of recently completed progressive houses is one Long Islander's way of understanding the place he comes from.

Timothy Godbold shares my fascination for modernism on the East End. From his Eugene Futterman–designed home in Southampton, New York, the interior designer founded the advocacy group Hamptons 20 Century Modern in 2020. But Godbold's perspective is squarely different from this writer's; born and raised in Australia, Godbold spread roots in the Hamptons after a vaunted career in fashion. To kick off this section, whose projects all have something to say about modernism's preservation or historical memory, I asked Tim to explain the appeal of the region's design legacy.

Were you drawn to America, or did you happen into living here?

As a little kid, I thought the full moon was America. I had a very glamorous auntie who lived in New York her whole life and ran a hair salon there. And I was always obsessed with American movies. Thinking back on being a kid who loved America, I think of modernism. I did not picture Dutch Colonial this or Mediterranean Revival that; America was quintessentially modernist.

Were the Hamptons part of this childhood understanding?

The Hamptons appeared on my radar when I was working for Ralph Lauren in London. The company would pull people from the Madison Avenue store to work in East Hampton for the summer, which wowed me. And because we had to copy the New York store windows in our respective locations, we would look to pictures of both the Madison Avenue and East Hampton windows as our templates. That was another aha moment. In those images, the perfectly manicured lawns and lined-up fences really fed into my OCD, and everything being awash in green was the opposite of dreary London in 1989.

You arrived in New York in 1995 and paid your first visit to East Hampton in 1996. Did the reality live up to the vision?

It was much more laid-back then—I felt you could walk in your bare feet. The investment bankers had just started coming back [after Black Monday and the recession of 1990–91], and there were still a lot of artists. There were more than a few houses like Grey Gardens. I was in awe of all of it.

The sheer volume of modern Hamptons houses really began to sink in later, in 2006, when your good friend purchased a house in the area.

I introduced her to her husband, so I almost had carte blanche to visit. That's when I could explore more extensively. My father was an architect. I also grew up in Perth, where every house on the coast looked like a Myron Goldfinger design. So, I had an instant connection to these Hamptons houses. I'm a cheerleader of the seventies and eighties because that's my childhood. But it's also because it's not mid-century modernism, and the vocabulary feels fresh. In my own design work now, I try to create a new vernacular based on everything I've lived in my life.

How did people respond to your initial enthusiasm?

There is still this feeling that seventies and eighties modernism is ugly, or at least not suited for the Hamptons. But what is suited, then? The illusion of class? I'm protective of these weird kids because I can relate to the weird kid.

It sounds like "weird" can be defined as "not midcentury." What differentiates the weird kids from the modernist local buildings that preceded them?

They're kind of perfect for beach environments, because they have big open spaces surrounded by a lot of glass. They're lighter and airier. Around that time, there was also a real striving to connect to nature, whether by employing stonework in interiors or configuring houses around planted courtyards. The flow between exterior and interior was layered.

I think you've got most of us beat when it comes to personal projects during COVID-19: you founded Hamptons 20 Century Modern just one month into the pandemic. Why this organization? Why now?

I had been thinking about it for a while, but the spark was that somebody had given me *The Houses of the Hamptons* by Paul Goldberger earlier in 2020. I posted a couple pictures from the book on Instagram, and someone I know said of the Norman Jaffe–designed Lloyd House, "Oh yeah, we pulled that one down last year." Totally blasé. That really upset me, and that's how the organization started. I had presumed there were conservation groups looking after these houses, but the reality was the opposite, so I decided to pick up the gauntlet, for better or for worse.

What are the first tasks of a newly formed preservation group?

We can't landmark the properties because we have a one-hundred-year preservation threshold currently. With the help of Alastair Gordon and others, we've pinned down thirty of the most important residences out here. Now I'm going to each town council and flagging those houses so that—should any of them ever come up for architectural review—the council members will know they are considering an important piece of architecture. It's sometimes hard to love the modernist house that has a lot of glass brick, weird corners and curves, and a not particularly thought-out interior in terms of closet space and bedroom sizes; that doesn't make it any less important. We need to look at these buildings and love them for what they are and the period during which they were built.

Casual observers sometimes conflate obsolete technology or visible aging with flawed design. Does that underlie people's resistance to preserving these houses?

Formica and faux everything really took off in the sixties, and they were fashion in the sense that they were treated disposably. Many of the houses had the technology without the craftsmanship. But these materials had a flair about them, perhaps because they weren't made expensively. When you're making a building out of cheaper materials, you can afford to be a bit more unconventional. That's another thing that distinguishes later modernism from midcentury modernism; there's more humor, more quirkiness. There's simply more boldness, too, which is more fun than academic modernism.

Acknowledging that you still have your own design practice to run, what comes next for Hamptons 20 Century Modern?

Everybody wants home tours. You can see houses on a computer all day long, but getting to experience these buildings in person is incredible. Ultimately, I'd like to see the Parrish Art Museum become the repository of all things Hamptons modernism. I also envision a learning annex dedicated to the subject—perhaps in a space at the Parrish, or better yet one of the houses themselves. I'd love for kids to get inspired by a direct experience with modernism, and even a place where they could study and practice design for a longer-term period.

What has been the greatest delight of your advocacy so far?

I keep discovering more houses and becoming more educated about the architects and designers of that period, which is also helping me connect to the Hamptons as my home. An even bigger thrill is going into the houses and hearing the excitement from people who own them or who bought them and did them up. I love hearing people's passion. It supports my argument that these houses are completely relevant and don't need to get demolished. You can update them and make them even more relevant.

And the most taxing?

Finding custodians for these houses. I'm not trying to keep any of this work to myself, and we're not going to be able to save anything without custodians—the more the merrier. But it almost feels like, if we can just get through the next five or ten years, people will start loving these houses like they love midcentury design. In the meantime, we need to protect as many of them as we can. Am I being Pollyannaish? I don't believe so. I think that people will realize that these buildings could have been built last year, and that they can serve their lives today equally well, in turn.

I think you're describing a positivity that has served you well personally—the spirit that catapulted you from Perth to London to New York, for instance.

When I started this project, I noticed that a lot of preservation-minded people were naysaying—talking about the good old days or being super-negative toward developers. My take is that you catch more flies with honey. Focusing on how amazing these buildings are—their lines, their materials—could spread the positivity. My dad would be so proud of me if he knew what I was doing. In my way, I do it in my father's name. I love living out here, and I love design. I think I'm a bit of shoplifter if I don't give back.

Interiors by Timothy Godbold, pictured right, include projects in Lower Manhattan (previous spread) as well as East Hampton and San Francisco, that are conversant in late modernism.

Antler House

Amagansett, New York

Two Street Studio

Thanks to the tireless work of filmmaker Jake Gorst, author Alastair Gordon, and others, Andrew Geller is finally being recognized as a defining voice in Long Island's modernism, rather than as a footnote. In the years leading up to 2019, Chris Fisher and Blair Moritz joined Geller's boosters with gusto. By preserving and sensitively adding on to Geller's 1968 Antler House in Springs, the couple invites a new generation of champions to appreciate the architect's contributions to midcentury design.

Fisher and Moritz initially stumbled into their stewardship roles. Circling the listing in 2014, the prospective buyers knew Geller's name was attached to the 1,200-square-foot house. But they also assumed that the place had been rendered irredeemable by thoughtless renovations and neglect. When closing the sale required demolishing a shed placed partly beyond the 1.1-acre property's setback, Fisher volunteered to take a sledgehammer to the structure. And just before he began swinging, he spotted a paper roll revealing signed diagrams made for Lawrence and Laura Antler.

The discovery prompted the clients to see the house's redeemability in a new light. They studied Geller's body of work as well as this commission's extant qualities, such as the way its layout and fenestration encouraged living among the treetops. As their admiration and sense of custodianship grew, Fisher and Moritz reached out to documentarian Gorst—Geller's grandson—who conveyed a full set of house plans to the new homeowners. Gorst also agreed to consult with Two Street Studio, the Brooklyn- and Virginia-based architecture firm that undertook this modernization project.

Two Street partner Forrest Frazier says, "Chris and Blair wanted to experience the house as it was intended," so the design team actively restored the most visible elevations to their original appearance and relegated expansions and niceties to places that passersby could not as easily see. The method allowed the collaborators to remove a recent, ill-conceived bathroom from the entryway, recreate Geller's "owl-eye" and triangular windows, and reinstall the interior entirely with cedar planks.

Examples of contemporary interventions include extending the rear of the house so that Two Street could split the ground-floor bathroom in two. The studio further created a carport with a rooftop deck that Geller had only penciled into the Antlers' drawings. To reconcile the long-ago sketch to Antler House in its current iteration, Frazier took a cue from the zigzagging roofline and shielded the deck stair behind a triangular plane. The deck balusters and carport screening are adapted directly from the original architect's own handrail detail.

From 1957 onward, Geller designed joyful, accessible coastal retreats at a pace that would have overwhelmed most anybody else—especially considering he also refused to repeat himself. Still, the architect did go through phases, and Antler House falls into what Gordon calls an "X-Acto period" in which rectilinear volumes were creased, folded, and sliced to resemble spacecrafts hovering above Tranquility Base. The inspiring revival of Antler House provides a fresh opportunity to better understand the time in which Geller practiced and to appreciate those accomplishments that are timeless: human scale, intimacy with nature, and architecture's ability to free one's spirit.

The exterior of Antler House intimates original architect Andrew Geller's captivation by the Space Race. "I think there's an ache for a smaller home like this, where the outdoor spaces feel like a continuation of the interior rooms," homeowner Chris Fisher says of Antler House's positive reception among neighbors.

"Geller gave a lot of thought to the sunrise and sunset, and to making sure that each room offers a different experience of the landscape," notes homeowner Blair Moritz. "The design is also a statement about living simply."

Montauk House

Montauk, New York

Rottet Studio

Andrew Geller, the midcentury architect introduced in the previous chapter, designed scores of houses for the East End while maintaining a full-time position at the legendary industrial design studio Raymond Loewy Associates. Geller's famed peer George Nelson shared that interest in multidisciplinary practice. This Montauk home now occupied by the contemporary multi-hyphenate architect Lauren Rottet was conceived by Nelson during the peak of his career as a designer of spaces, furnishings, and graphics.

In another similarity to Geller, Nelson found inspiration in Long Island. In 1956, Nelson and Gordon Chadwick—with whom he often shared architect credits—had designed a shingle-clad East Hampton house as a reinterpretation of the town's late-Victorian Shingle Style buildings. The 1961 house that the collaborators designed for Rudolph and Ethel Johnson in Montauk was also covered in shingles, but as Rottet points out of her summer residence, here the composition of hexagonal shapes resembles a deconstruction of the early-nineteenth-century smock windmill, of which there are several surviving examples locally.

Nelson and Chadwick had crafted the residence for another site nearby, but after changing hands and a series of unfortunate renovations, the pair's intent was nearly lost. To preserve the one-of-a-kind home, in 1989 the Johnsons' son Richard hired the original contractor to construct a near-exact reproduction on an acre perched above Lake Montauk. The younger Johnson sold his 2,700-square-foot phoenix to artists Jonathan Horowitz and Rob Pruitt, from whom Rottet acquired the residence in 2012.

Since then, Rottet has updated the house with the care and passion of an ostensible member of the Johnson family. Some improvements—such as replacing cedar shingles and oak flooring or threading air-conditioning through the structure—are barely visible to today's visitor. Other interventions are more substantial, albeit entirely sympathetic to Nelson and Chadwick's vision. These include the reconfiguration of a mechanical room and workshop into a guest suite, insertion of sliding doors on the southwest elevation, and the addition of a saltwater pool adjacent to those sliders. Simultaneously, Rottet amassed midcentury furnishings over innumerable local outings, and she combined them with her own designs as well as artworks by Alexander Calder, Larry Poons, and Kiki Smith. Nelson's iconic Marshmallow Sofa (designed with Irving Harper), a Paul McCobb credenza, and other vintage pieces came with the house.

"This house is a prime example of the incredibly creative progression of modernist design, and I am so grateful to have the responsibility of carrying on the story," Rottet reflects, adding that stewardship has yielded insights about her own creative practice. "Working within hexagonal rooms forces you to think outside the metaphorical box of right angles and rectangles that designers are taught in school. It encourages you to explore interior space from a new perspective, as the angles collectively amount to nearly 360-degree views and a seemingly endless indoor-outdoor experience." Rottet's most recent Montauk Collection, in which furniture doubles as art, pays subtle tribute to Nelson as well as the Johnsons and their colorful successors.

Montauk House's formal entry faces the rear of the property. It is fronted by a cedar shingle-clad ramp that accesses the kitchen, as well as a two-story volume whose ground-floor guest suite was once a mechanical room and workshop.

Kitting out the residence, architect-homeowner Lauren Rottet combined original millwork, a full-height dining-room screen, and other extant details with midcentury finds, a decades-spanning art collection, and furnishings of her own design. Rottet also spearheaded fundamental interventions, like the addition of a saltwater pool.

Six Square House

Bridgehampton, New York

Young Projects

The Bridgehampton property that Colleen Foster shares with Chris Canavan and their son was once an either-or kind of place. Inside the circa-1865 main residence, you could either knit yourself into household life around the living room's hearth or banish yourself to a peripheral room. Thanks to a rear barn building that had bisected the backyard, you could either hem to the charming Victorian or escape detection at the pool in the way back.

Canavan says the physical environment had emotional consequences. "If Colleen were to go to the pool, she would feel that she had removed herself from the family," he cites as an example. The couple also observed that the setup fostered a less-than-ideal dynamic among overnight guests, who felt obliged to stay close to the living room—which in turn pressured their hosts into choreographing activities with machine-like precision. To Foster and Canavan, modernizing and expanding the residence could provide the fix. He adds, "When we brought in Bryan, our driving force was to have a place where you could be independent but not excommunicated, where you could interact over a weekend or holiday without feeling too structured."

Bryan refers to Bryan Young, principal of Young Projects. "I've always been attracted to the agricultural economy of the Hamptons and concerned about its displacement," Foster says of hiring the progressive Brooklyn-based design studio. "We wanted to respect that history, but we also wanted something inventive."

Young confirmed the couple's suspicion that the barn had an adverse impact on the quality of living, and he concluded that that outweighed its historical value. Young Projects proposed replacing the unplumbed structure with 3,500 square feet of ground-up construction, which would become the homeowners' primary venue; they could flow between the new building and the Victorian house on typical days, and turn the nineteenth-century residence completely over to guests on crowded weekends and holidays.

Taking into consideration zoning setbacks as well as the locations of mature trees and stormwater paths, the design team sited a new building approximately in the same middle ground as the old barn. Even so, the project is pushed as close to the one-and-a-half-acre lot's southern boundary as possible, so that it would triangulate with the Victorian and pool instead of separating them. Now the property feels like a campus, where one can simultaneously enjoy long views across the landscape as well as a sense of cohesion. "There are three or four or even five focal points across the entire property, which to me is really invigorating," Canavan says. "Each has a center of gravity, yet you're not separated." Young further observes, "You are also bearing witness to a historical dialogue, as you see the contemporary and Victorian houses tempering and relating to one another."

The new home also embodies a memory of the barn. Paying homage to the shape of the demolished outbuilding, Young Projects conceived a gabled structure that measures twenty-four feet square, and then multiplied that module by six to accommodate a program that includes two bedrooms, full kitchen and dining areas, and three multipurpose living areas, as well as a freestanding garage and a separate, semi-enclosed volume for outdoor entertaining. The parking structure stands slightly apart from the other five volumes, separated by a meandering walkway that accesses a shade garden along the south side of the building.

The five inhabitable volumes are huddled in a star formation around a triangular courtyard. Young poses that the fundamental squares could "repeat infinitely to accommodate program." Moreover, the modules are not just arranged around this outdoor space; they press into one another, and their classic gabled forms are dramatically modified for the arrangement. Whereas the freestanding garage maintains the rectilinear base, centered ridge, and forty-five-degree roof planes of an identifiably rural structure, its counterparts share a roof that circumscribes the courtyard by way of undulating eaves. Canavan suggests thinking about the composition as "magnetic," noting, "If you really mashed it together, each constituent part could no longer declare itself a barn."

To meld the volumes, Young Projects aligned the individual modules' ridges by way of shifting and rotation and then employed arcing roof eaves as the connective tissue. Accoya wood is fashioned into slats to negotiate the sweeping exterior geometry. Young adds that a different series of arcs were applied to the underside of the roof, so that ceilings blend into one another; much like the campus plan, the interior layout threads a needle of togetherness and personal autonomy. "The modules interact with each other to create something unexpected and discrete at the outer perimeter, while having continuity within the interior," the architect says of the difference between the roofscape and ceiling planes. Of the overall scheme, he adds, "The simplicity of the geometry and clarity of the structural logic is borne of respect for the historic barn, but it feeds into something more dynamic than a 'modern barn.'"

Young's reference to dynamism could refer to any number of effects: the way the huddled formation inspires someone to circle the new house and explore its grounds, rather than forthrightly enter inside; or the way each module frames different views of the landscape and embodies different attitudes about the Hamptons. The site offers much to ponder about pedigree—Young cites Louis Kahn's Dominican Motherhouse and the formation of salt crystals as equal influences—and about architecture as an act of both abiding and defying tradition.

Considering that Young Projects wrapped work in 2021, these meanings will take time to coalesce. The appeal of the finished product, on the other hand, has been immediate. Canavan delights in the spatial relationships and material dialogues that seem to continually reveal themselves, while Foster concludes, "While I knew Bryan was creating something of beauty, this project is in fact a thing of surprise and significance that I hadn't expected."

Six Square House strikes many balances.
It surprises the eye while exuding calm; it
is a personal escape that also contributes
significantly to Bridgehampton's heritage; the
design can stoke nesting or intellectualizing.
The Young Projects–designed residence
is surrounded by a landscape designed by
Minneapolis-based Coen+Partners.

Watermill Residence

Water Mill, New York

Roger Ferris + Partners

Since completing a golf club facility in Bridge-hampton in 2008, architect Roger Ferris has been a constant presence in the East End. Westport, Connecticut–based Roger Ferris + Partners' works in the Hamptons include a diaphanous hotel addition and residential commissions as varied as sleek beachfront houses and cheeky meditations on the American Dream. Today the studio also operates from an office in Bridgehampton.

While Ferris demurs to the idea of being personally influential, when pressed on the matter, he thinks his philosophy strikes a chord with homeowners. "I'm interested in lyrical buildings that have some resonance of familiarity," he says, adding, "I think of building projects as prayers, by which I mean opportunities to control or manifest meaning. This is a particularly maddening time for everyone, which underscores the search and the need to resolve something, somewhere." Ferris's method is also noteworthy in that he starts a project by writing a narrative based on client interviews, saving drawing for later. The diversity of Ferris's East End buildings is almost incidental to the way the architect and his clients gel initially and collaborate thereafter.

Indeed, the vibe was immediate with Matthew and Nicole Ammirati. The husband and wife had purchased a 3,100-square-foot house in Water Mill designed by the prolific late-midcentury Hamptons architect Norman Jaffe, and Ferris was the first contemporary practitioner the couple had encountered who did not view the 1980 residence as a teardown. He proposed an ostensible restoration of the four-bedroom house, with subtle tweaks and updates. "The antiquity is still there, the sculptural quality is still intact, but it's found a new equilibrium," Ferris explains of the project's vision. "It's a restoration that shouldn't burden the homeowners with a sense of history."

Restorative tasks included dismantling and numbering the interior cedar panels, for sanding and reinstallation in the renovation's finish stages. Ferris also replaced the house's windows through the original manufacturer and specified exterior cedar according to the original design.

To establish that new equilibrium, Roger Ferris + Partners refined the interior detailing, about which Ferris says, "I don't think Jaffe overly cared about negotiating the meeting between two dissimilar materials, which are some things I tried to attend to." He also introduced several new materials—polished concrete for the sunken living room's floor and engineered stone surfaces lining bathrooms, for instance—while subtly pushing at the size and proportion of rooms in the process. "I suspect Jaffe would have done this himself if he were here and knew how design and materiality had progressed up to this point. I say the objective for the house was to make it more Jaffe than Jaffe, though perhaps this is exactly what he would have created today."

The divining of perspective bespeaks a profound respect for Jaffe, who drowned off the coast of Bridgehampton in 1993. It was this same esteem that propelled Ferris's "reticent" design of two small freestanding structures northwest of the residence. Serving as a pool house and garage, the volumes quietly evoke Jaffe's handling of solid and void, but as rectilinear volumes clad in blackened wide-plank cedar, they remain largely deferential to the sculptural main house.

"Adding contemporary elements to an existing building creates a kind of duality that underscores the passage of time. But I didn't want to create some radical gesture here. These black buildings figuratively occupy the shadow of Jaffe's work, and they reinforce the horizontal datum of the main house," Ferris says of his intervention. The architect observes that, in addition to creating a visually connected compound, the pair of additions guides the Ammiratis' relationship with the site, which measures just under an acre. Namely, the buildings frame a view of the existing pool and direct one's attention to open fields that border the property to the west.

Asked to compare the creative satisfaction of this commission to one of his East End projects that springs fully from the ground, Ferris agrees that all-new construction might seem more fulfilling. But upon closer scrutiny, "trying to understand the essence of what came before—and how to both embrace and transform it—is intellectually and artistically challenging." The process is also inevitably educational, allowing Ferris to deeply consider Jaffe's method of designing almost cave-like spaces around which he formed a referential yet iconic enclosure. "I think you can't help but get tattooed to some degree by working on these things."

Watermill Residence encompasses a 1980 main residence designed by Norman Jaffe and meticulously restored and updated by architect Roger Ferris's eponymous firm, as well as all-new pool house and garage pavilions.

Sag Harbor House

Sag Harbor, New York

Ted Porter Architecture

When New York–based architect Ted Porter was growing up in northern Mississippi, visits to his grandparents meant reading and rereading the same issue of *House Beautiful* that an aunt had once left behind in the guest bedroom. Yet the lone, dog-eared magazine happened to contain a project that was worth coming back to: a Norman Jaffe–designed house on the edge of Wainscott, New York, that remixed the traditional shingle saltbox into a modernist revelation. While the write-up did not point the young Porter toward architecture—he already knew about the profession and that New York City was where he wanted to practice it—it added a layer to the vision of his future. City people went to a place called the Hamptons to celebrate nature and creativity.

By the time Porter was ready to shuttle between New York and the East End himself, Jaffe's vision still captured his imagination. But the twin desires of a walkable neighborhood and a sheltered patch of garden outweighed the appeal of tending the kind of remotely located modernist house that had inspired Porter as a child. He and his longtime partner, Steve Godeke, in turn felt drawn to Sag Harbor at a time when the former whaling village was beginning its inexorable pull into the Hamptons' orbit. In 1999, they purchased Sag Harbor House, a then-eighty-year-old gambrel-roofed cottage located on a quarter-acre lot near downtown.

When the couple decided to extensively update the 1,900-square-foot residence in 2015, the architect had abundant site-specific knowledge and professional expertise to act upon. However charming, Sag Harbor's vintage houses were low-ceilinged and poorly illuminated, and Porter desired greater interaction with the outdoors. He laughingly admits, too, that a gut renovation could yield a well-deserved coat closet.

The building's contributing status within the landmarked Sag Harbor Village District forced the architect-homeowner to work largely within the existing footprint and envelope. Government oversight further meant that he could make just a few, historically sensitive improvements to its front elevation. Yet, in Porter's hands, these parameters were by no means limiting. By utilizing the attic volume and replacing the existing straight stair with an intricately conceived switchback, he opened the interior dramatically. These moves most notably allowed him to raise the second floor, so that the living room's ceiling could exceed ten feet; a monumental, triple-glazed window within the rear, northeast-facing elevation floods the living room with diffuse daylight and overlooks the carefully tended garden. Porter also added five feet of width to the rear screened porch and surmounted it with an enclosed sunroom. In a nod to the interiors of Jaffe's Wainscott commission, he clad all rooms entirely in white oak planks.

Modernism comes in many different packages. The newfound capaciousness and indoor-outdoor quality of Sag Harbor House shows that even dense, highly regulated environments can accommodate the movement's principles. In fact, they are made richer by the conjoining of past and present.

Rear-facing interventions in the home that
architect Ted Porter shares with Steve Godeke
in the Sag Harbor Village District, which first
earned historic-district status in 1973. Without
altering the building's public identity, Porter
oversaw a complete dismantling of the interior
and then reconfigured it into a gracious series of
modern rooms.

House in the Dunes

Amagansett, New York

Worrell Yeung

Max Worrell and Jejon Yeung have been pretty much inseparable since their first day of Yale student orientation in 2004. Although the architects knew almost as quickly that they would be partners in business as well as life, they waited a decade to formalize that professional commitment. The launch of Brooklyn-based Worrell Yeung in 2014 was in part catalyzed that same year by a request from longtime friends to modernize the Charles Gwathmey–designed Haupt Residence in Amagansett.

The homeowners had a pristine artifact on their hands, having just purchased the 1978 house from the son of Gwathmey's original client. "They were very passionate about the house. They loved that it hadn't been touched, and they were really dedicated to preserving it," Worrell says of his and Yeung's friends. "In this project, our touch was delicate, because we all took a lot of care with how it would be read."

The renovation, completed in phases over four years, replaced all building systems, including the cedar-clad envelope and adjacent pool deck. Worrell Yeung re-created the exterior during this process, with a focus on the weathertightness and energy efficiency of doors and windows.

The studio took a slightly less faithful approach to the 4,400-square-foot interior. Most notable among its interventions is a kitchen reconfiguration that opens fully to adjacent living and dining areas. Worrell Yeung also identified a disconnectedness in the original primary bath suite, where a walk-in closet, with integrated makeup vanity, consumed more space than the bathroom itself. "That didn't work for how people live today," Worrell says of formulating a response; now the suite is reconfigured in the same footprint to include a larger shower, a freestanding bathtub, and still-generous storage.

Striking an appropriate balance between preservation and adaptation demanded a "fluid" dialogue between architect and client, Yeung says. "There would be moments when we would advocate against changing something too dramatically and the response would be, 'We have to make the house our own.' And there were other moments when they thought our modification pushed too hard against precedent."

Not all conversations centered on maximizing functionality for the homeowners. In some cases, the collaborators tried imagining how Gwathmey might navigate the resources available in the marketplace today. Yeung thinks the modernist would have embraced this project's kitchen appliances because they reinforce the architecture in ways that their clunky predecessors could not. In another example, Worrell astutely points out that switching eight-inch recessed can lighting with white baffles "makes the house feel calm and fresh—though I admit that that could be a commentary on how our generation perceives an older technology." The architects eliminated a whimsical oak element from the fireplace wall deemed out of character for Gwathmey-designed beach houses of this period, and they simultaneously removed flanking built-in bookcases to make room for art. Back in the kitchen, they reinterpreted the erstwhile laminate countertops in slightly less modest engineered stone edged in oak. The latter upgrade was also meant to keep pace with Amagansett's present-day toniness, though Worrell says that erring too far on the side of luxury "would have felt wrong conceptually."

Yeung notes the result of these efforts continues to read like a composition by Gwathmey, whose 1960s- and 1970s-era East End houses fundamentally shifted the vocabulary of contemporary residential design. Of this body of work, he adds, "Spatially it is very complex, where the continuity between interior and the outdoors and the volumizing of circulation are not immediately understandable." Reflecting specifically on the Haupt Residence's place in history, Worrell also observes how "Gwathmey played with section in such interesting, seemingly unpredictable ways, shifting volumes and grabbing daylight. Experiencing this house powerfully shifts your perception of space." That statement is certainly true for Worrell Yeung itself. Ushering the Haupt Residence into the twenty-first century has influenced the up-and-coming studio's crafting of environments during the formative stages of its development. Worrell Yeung's current slate of commissions—in the Hamptons as well as farther afield—more enthusiastically embraces the kind of visible subversion and ingenuity that made Charles Gwathmey one of the foremost architects of his generation.

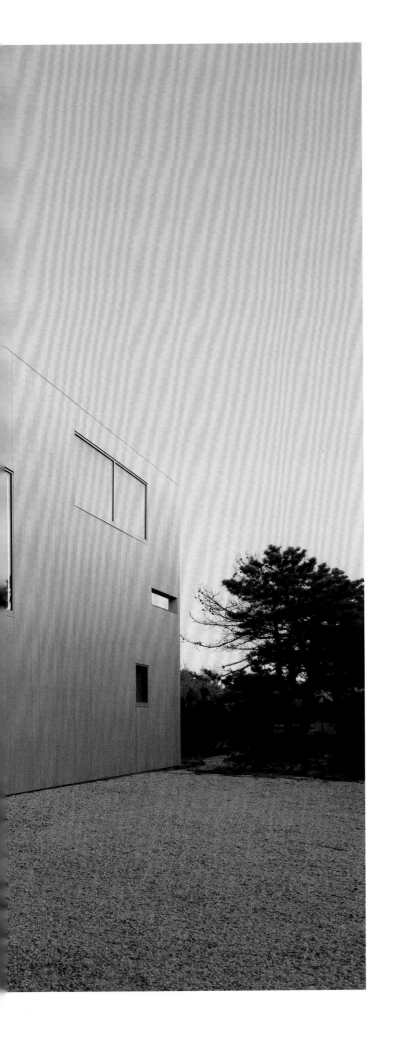

For House in the Dunes, Worrell Yeung sensitively shepherded the Haupt Residence—an Amangansett home designed by Charles Gwathmey and his partner Robert Siegel in 1978—into the present day.

In the magazine's 1979 survey of the year's best houses, *Architectural Record* stated, "the Haupt house had to be raised ten feet over mean high water or four and a half feet over existing grade. This produced the opportunity for a series of half levels that the architects exploited with skill. The half levels are linked by a series of stepped ramps that zone apart owners and guest bedrooms both vertically and horizontally."

Extending the Legacy

Q&A with Nick Martin

Nick Martin's 1996 visit to Westhampton, New York, didn't go quite as planned. Instead of passing through on his way to a new life in Milan, the architect settled in, first finding work with architects James Merrell and Frederick Stelle and subsequently opening an eponymous studio in 2000. Since then, Martin's projects have included sensitive renovations to East End homes that were designed by several generations of progressive architects—among them Eugene Futterman, Norman Jaffe, Alfred De Vido, Smith-Miller + Hawkinson, and his personal mentor Charles Gwathmey. Martin also works in all-new construction, and these designs likewise adapt the spirit of the region's twentieth-century modernism to the circumstances of our time.

In other words, Martin is ideally suited for the conversation that kicks off "Extending the Legacy." Thanks to his previous relationships and renovation portfolio, as well as his queue of ground-up projects, Martin has devoted significant thought to the forces that have shaped East End modernism over decades. He is, moreover, navigating shifts in financing, regulation, and attitude so they become features of his work rather than limitations. As you progress from the interview to individual project descriptions, Martin's reflections should reverberate. In this section of *Hamptons Modern*, contemporary architects actively engage with a historical continuum according to their personal values, clients' priorities, and site specificities.

Commissions by architect Nick Martin, shown here and on the following spread, include an almost imperceptible, yet transformative renovation of the Charles Gwathmey–designed Tolan House, as well as an Amangansett residence dubbed Of Good Water and the forthcoming Azurest Legacy in Sag Harbor.

In this book's introductory essay, I remark on the ubiquity of modernism on the East End. Without splitting hairs about derivative designs, why do you think progressive architectural language has gone mainstream out here?

Midcentury houses were built for summer living, and they were emblematic of a postwar culture that was ready for new things. Even though the building environment is different today, I think the seasonal quality of an East End home allows that modernist heritage to continue to unfold. For many clients, these are second and even third residences. Consequently they can let go of some of the traditional signifiers of home—the clients allow these houses to represent a life that is lived more actively, and with purpose.

Was there a moment when you realized that modernism was no longer fringe?

I remember attending a holiday party in a relatively modest house that had just been renovated in a deliberately modern way. When you see smaller, grassroots projects embracing a point of view, then you know that there is genuine appeal for that movement.

Thinking about your renovations of twentieth-century houses, what opportunities are made available to you by interacting with these buildings so intimately?

We're reimagining a large Futterman house in Sagaponack with the original client. The owners are a wonderful, creative couple with a passion for understanding architecture. Working with them has been a gift.

Have you been able to expand your nuts-and-bolts understanding of regional modernism through this work, too?

There is learning through renovating. The way that Charlie Gwathmey's forms define positive and negative spaces, or how they balance transparency versus opacity, reminds me of the first principles of my architecture education. For each project, Charlie would also use a grid based on Le Corbusier's original module, and we would design everything according to that grid. When I worked on the Tolan House, it was like Charlie was right next to me again, like we were following and breaking that grid together.

Would you identify some of the forces that have shaped East End architecture more recently? For instance, building science wields much more influence on houses today.

That's accurate. We went from a society of summer lodging to one focused on year-round residency—and now full-time residency, considering COVID-19. The original modernist houses were not designed with HVAC or even insulation. Those technologies are obligatory now as building departments are requiring a base level of green practices.

The regulatory environment has become stricter in general.

I'm reminded of a Montauk project in which a height moratorium came into play. The regulation helped define the architecture. Working within regulations and restraints can create the rhythm, the *parti*, or even the culture of a house. I find that the site, environment, sun angle, and client's scope and point of view allow each house to be unique if the designer's mind can listen.

Socially, too, this part of the world has changed rather dramatically. It's no longer a playground for artists.

I would say that there are still currents of invention and artistry. However, this place is now home to some of the world's top earners, which is reflected in the architecture marketplace. Compared to when I first arrived here, market saturation has created intense competition for residential commissions.

How do you recruit younger people into your studio? It's difficult to live on the North or South Fork on an associate's salary today.

That's an important consideration, and funnily enough, I just purchased a new office building in Bridgehampton for which I'm designing three upstairs apartments for younger employees. Zoom is a fine platform for established architects, and those architects can live farther away from the studio. But it's critical to have younger people by your side. I also believe that, when you put real effort into a person's growth, young or otherwise, he or she blossoms and returns the favor in a high degree.

Essentially, what we're talking about is mentorship and presence. If we think of ourselves as mentors and teachers, rather than focusing on fees and deadlines, then the process unfolds smoothly. When everyone feels that the studio is a place of continual learning and growth, then ethics and focus prevail. For our practice, those priorities are environmental advocacy, knowledge of materials and how they work together, and community understanding.

What new positions would you like East End architecture to stake?

I would love to take emphasis off computer-driven constraints and return to practicing architecture with more playfulness, more effort devoted to geometry, more dialogue with vernacular, material, engineering, and tonal expressions. I also find that the cultural conversation about design has become too centered on trends, to the detriment of finding solutions in a more athletic way.

You often speak of practicing architecture like a watercolorist. Could you explain that?

An oil painting is something that you can work and rework to perfection. In watercolor, the wash is bright and transparent, and the mark of the brush is evident from start to finish. I do push for watercolor-like architecture, where fresh ideas and energy manifest in the built work.

Could you talk about your project Azurest Legacy? This forthcoming single-family residence is located in the historically Black neighborhood Azurest, which came to light for many people in Colson Whitehead's 2009 novel *Sag Harbor*.

Working on that project is as important as working on a Norman Jaffe house because you're considering an important local legacy that must be saved. I wanted to honor this legacy by finding an architectural vocabulary that respects the neighborhood and its vintage buildings, but which also resonates as *architecture* with a capital A. Our inventive client, who is first-generation Ethiopian American, believes in design as a medium for both cultural meaning and creativity. Using that blend of criteria, we landed on a bridge-like structure and an interior courtyard scheme that minimize the impact on the existing trees and undergrowth and allows us to bring in more native plants. It's been a great study, she's a great client, and we're really enjoying the process of reinventing the vernacular.

How does sustainability figure into East End modernism, or your work specifically?

I've always been concerned by humans' effect on the land, and educating the client about environmental impact is such a meaningful part of our process. For example, I think passive design strategies have to inform every project; comfort does not have to rely on mechanical engineering alone. I also believe in sourcing local materials and craftsmanship, because that makes a home more of its place. And it is possible to convince clients to reduce their square footage, especially when you can show that many of the existing spaces they love are smaller than they realize. I try to teach these values through positivity.

My father has had an illustrious life. When he visits me, he says, "These people you work for, their lifestyle doesn't match reality anywhere. How do you hold on to your moral compass?" I think the answer has to do with aligning with clients who have similar values, who feel passionate about the environment and about invention.

This sparks a question about spec development. It has been steamrolling through the East End since the postwar period, but observers find it especially egregious nowadays. What are your thoughts on the subject?

Spec development is like the manufacturing of a typical car. People do need cars, but mass production represents a loss of potential. A meadow or field that is transformed into twenty built lots represents twenty missed opportunities for young creative minds and young tradespeople to come into their own and express what their clients can be. Architecture, as a product and a process, can make a genuine difference in one's life.

Redwood Residence

Sag Harbor, New York

Hal Goldstein

"My only interest is articulating volume as well as the character of a room: where does the light come from? what is the smell of the room? what is the touch of the materials? I want to photograph the air in a room."

This is how Scott Frances describes his approach to photographing architecture and interiors. Frances's commitment to documenting space as well as atmosphere may be difficult to describe in concise terms, but its resonance is quite easy to sum up. For more than three decades, a who's who of designers, hoteliers, and developers have relied on Frances to shoot their projects.

In 2016, Frances and spouse Patti Weinberg turned the tables on the design world, when they decided to purchase a neglected midcentury residence boasting a northern view of the Big Narrows in Sag Harbor. Thanks to Frances's hard-earned renown, the couple could have chosen any number of talents to create a new residence for the hilltop site. Thinking back on his client roster, Frances says that photography sessions for architect Hal Goldstein struck a chord. "Hal's working from the inside out made a big impression on me in terms of materials, furniture placement, and the quality of light; he really thought about living within a house," the photographer recalls. Frances invited Goldstein to walk the site, where Weinberg, struck by the architect's enthusiasm and collaborative spirit, approved the choice.

Just as quickly, the trio determined to build at the highest point of the property, nearest to the parcel's southwest corner. Weinberg also established one of the major parameters for Goldstein's design. Reflecting on her and her husband's lack of ostentation, as well as their mutual desire to someday age in place, she requested a "one-story home with character and soul. My big thing with Hal was that I didn't want to live in a two-dimensional image."

Goldstein, whose company HGX Design operates from studios in New York and Bridgehampton, embedded texture into the design at several scales. He tucked a garage into the twelve-foot rise and arranged three thousand square feet into three low-slung volumes on the hillock's crest. These three parts assume a U shape. Guest rooms occupy the easternmost volume, which tops the garage, while the primary bedroom suite is held within a second volume, not visible from the street, that faces the guest wing across a courtyard. The volume connecting them stands slightly toward the north and includes the main entry on its east face. That front door opens to a twelve-foot-tall interior where a kitchen, dining area, and living room meld into one

another, and a den partly hides behind the fireplace wall; all common spaces share a sixty-foot-long expanse of windows overlooking the fescue that swirls immediately outside and the Narrows in the distance.

Detailing distinguishes one volume from the other and adds a more intimate layer of character to the exterior composition. A steady rhythm of beams crowning the public rooms punctuate the building envelope to cradle the roof, for example, and the cedar that clads their exterior walls is largely installed as vertical planks. Meanwhile, the flanking volumes sport cedar shiplap, though all these configurations are rotated ninety degrees wherever facades surround an operable window. Inside, a similar logic rules. Distinctions of height and finish signal one's location within the plan, without compromising continuity between the three zones. Weinberg is still visibly excited by Goldstein's mastery of materials, and Frances praises Goldstein for eschewing a process "that insists on a heroic stair or fireplace to anchor a photograph. Here, everything is informed by everything else."

Goldstein partly credits his research for the accomplishment. At this project's outset, the architect reviewed the inherently humble-yet-sophisticated World War II–era cottages that the likes of Marcel Breuer and Paul Weidlinger designed for themselves on Cape Cod. Although Sag Harbor's whaling history drove him to study the Massachusetts peninsula for references, he also reasoned that there was more inspiration to be found in one of America's first test beds of Bauhaus expression than in the Hamptons, where early modernist principles had been adapted and reinterpreted over two interceding generations. Goldstein adds that the simplicity of historical modernism strikes a personal chord. "I always think about taking architecture only as far as it needs to go," he says, "so you don't have to do another thing."

That contemplation didn't take long. In mid-2018, Frances and Weinberg began moving in their belongings, combining their twentieth-century furnishings, multi-era artworks, and travel discoveries to almost startling effect. "I experienced such surprise when Scott sent me his first photographs of the unpacked spaces. What a gift to realize that he and Patti were keeping all these wonderful things in mind as they made decisions." By not having to do another thing, Goldstein allowed his clients to exercise the creative license they so clearly possess.

While Redwood Residence was palpably influenced by first generation East Coast modernism, the design by Hal Goldstein includes twenty-first-century flourishes like a mirrored backsplash that inserts landscape reflections into the kitchen. The ease with which homeowners Scott Frances and Patti Weinberg filled the space with their personal finds is a testament to the close collaboration between architect and client.

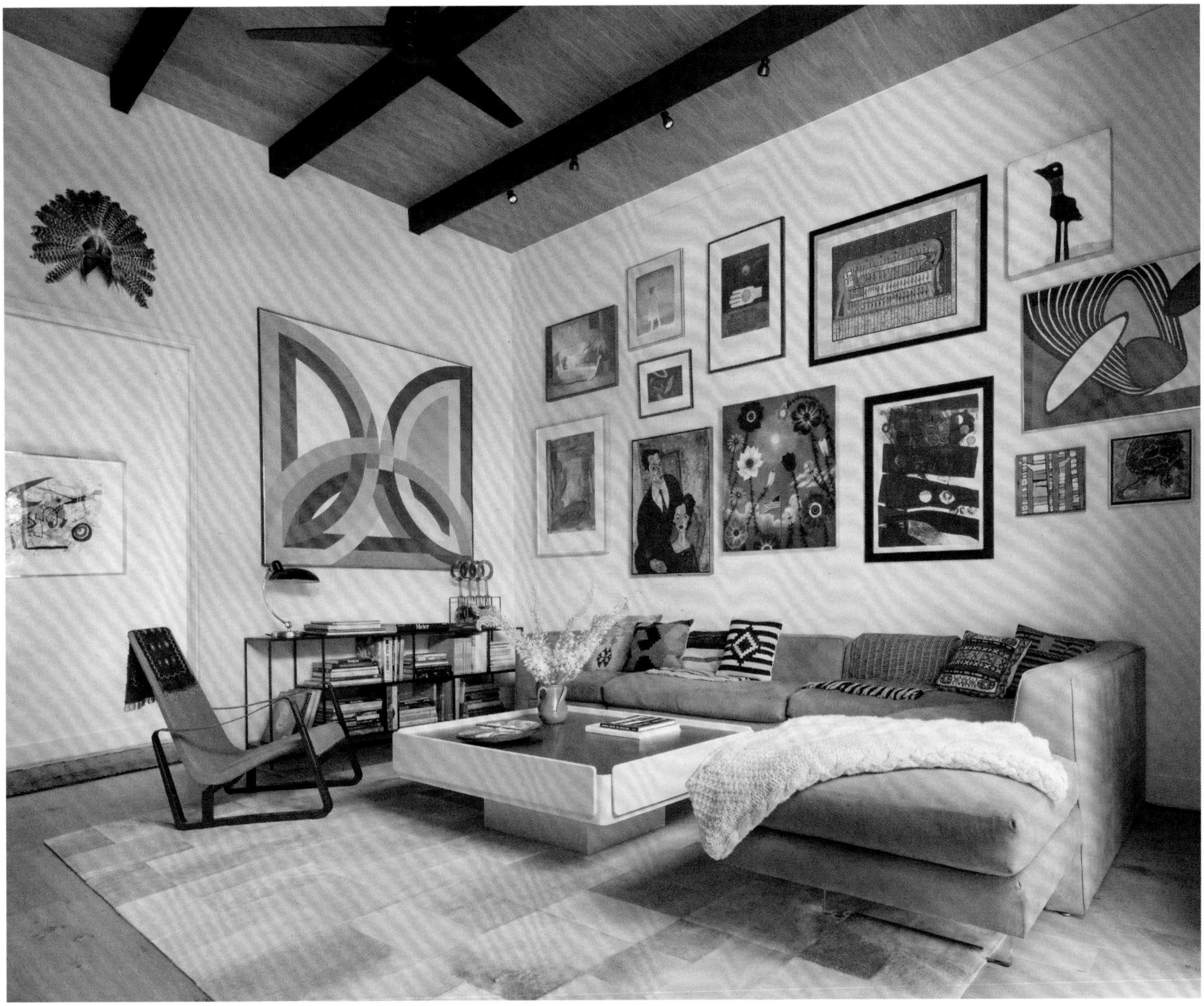

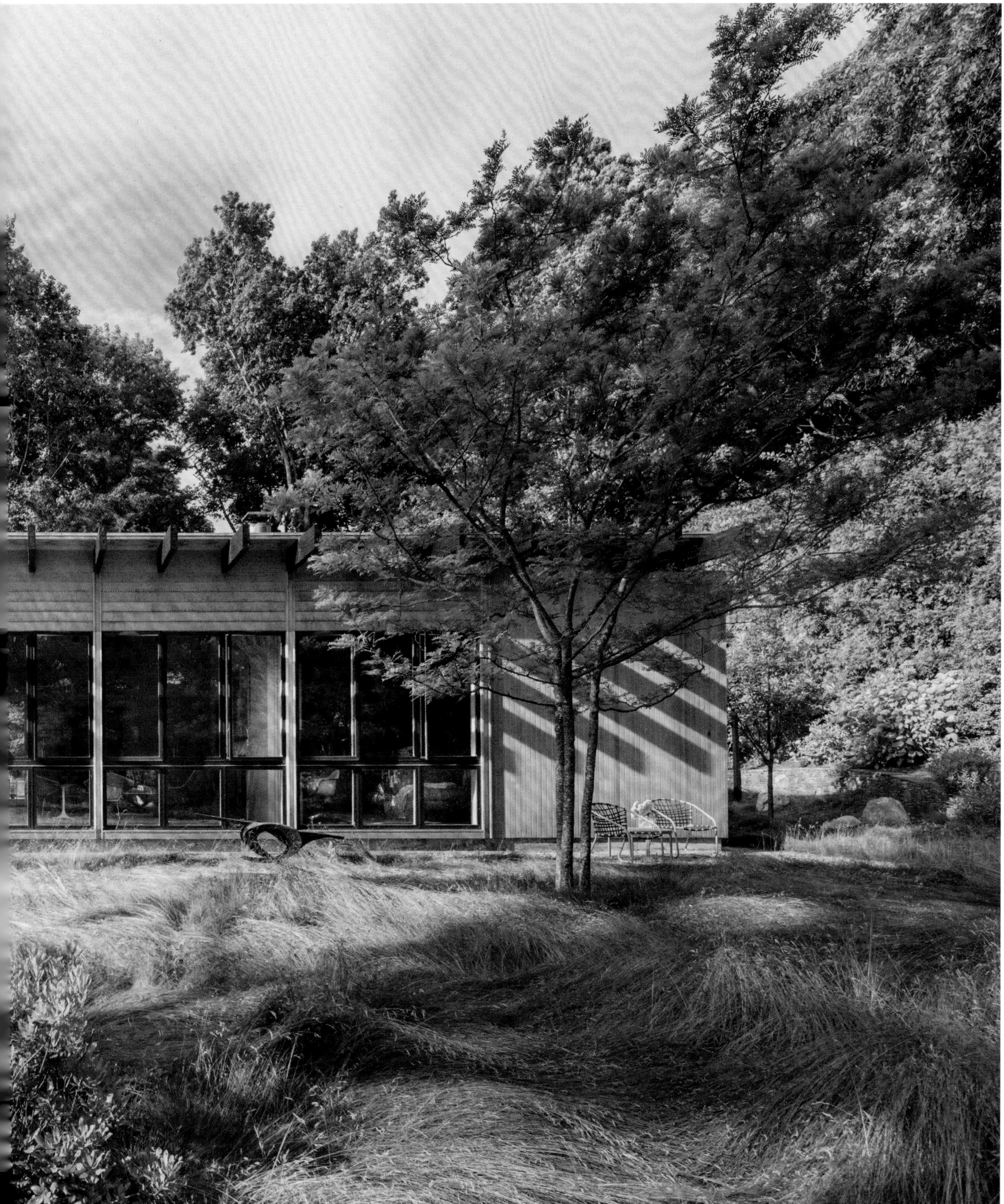

Bellport House

Bellport, New York

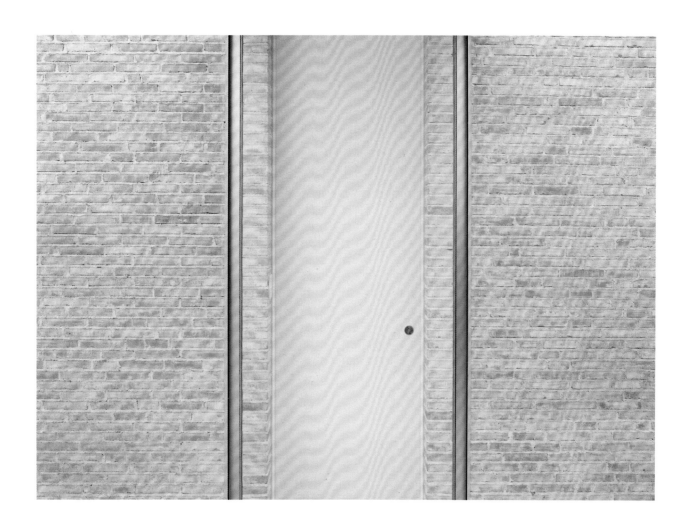

toshihiro oki architect

This handsome and thought-provoking home in Bellport was commissioned by a couple that includes a dignitary of New York's modern art market. Yet do not presume that an art-world client champions visual invention above all other criteria. In fact, as New York–based architect Toshihiro Oki recalls from the design process, the building's form was almost incidental to the active social life it had to support.

Completed in 2018, Bellport House was erected on the footprint of a 1960s-era residence that the client had occupied for several years prior to tapping Oki for a collaboration. That the husband and wife had a long-standing relationship with the building and its uniquely wide parcel overlooking Bellport Bay meant they were also clear-eyed about what a replacement project needed to accomplish. Foremost among those goals was the ability to accommodate a rotating cast of weekend guests as well as larger one-off events. They additionally favored expanses of glass that would celebrate the connectivity between earth and water; the husband, an avid boater, also opposed embedding these windows and sliding doors within wood siding, knowing that the material would demand continual upkeep in the briny atmosphere.

Although Bellport House is mercifully situated on fast-draining soil at one of the highest points along the village's bay, coastal construction is strongly regulated as a matter of course. In turn, architect and client agreed to reuse the existing 4,400-square-foot, half-pinwheel-shaped footprint to spare their project from some time-consuming review. The collaborators then iterated numerous plans within that outline, which traces the shore's southwest–northeast axis, to create the best configuration for entertaining. A collection of large, almost-public-scale spaces fills the figurative pinwheel's rotor, and a swimming pool nestles into its bayside crook. Four bedrooms are pushed to the plan's outer limits, and at the westernmost point, a fifth bedroom encompasses the only second-story space in the house: a four-hundred-square-foot contemporary interpretation of the widow's walk.

At the very center of the rotor area, a pair of rooms captures the environmental and social ambitions of this project in a nutshell. The generous entry is faced almost entirely in glass on the front and rear elevations so that this receiving area also functions as a lens to the landscape. A warming kitchen and basement stair tucked behind the adjacent hallway bespeaks the hustling of serving pieces in and out of storage and the readying of refreshments for passing around.

The bedrooms also deserve closer scrutiny, given that they represent the extent to which Oki got into the heads of visitors and their gracious hosts. By hemming the bedrooms to the edges of the house plan and organizing them with en suite bathrooms, the architect encourages users to think of their rooms as retreats. Oki amplified the getaway sensibility by articulating the building perimeter so that each bedroom accesses a different outdoor scene; he further employed flange-like partition walls and entry stairs to extend into, and section off, the landscape. If there is a rhythm to a typical weekend trip, then this treatment of bedrooms makes the adagios possible for guests and hosts alike.

Tonal, irregularly coursed brick facades, as well as a retractable shaded roof deck and a chain-link trellis, lend a casual air to Bellport House's disciplined form and expansive glass walls.

The residence's upper story is accessed just beyond the cook's kitchen, where stainless-steel monoliths are a source of both visual gravity and reflected daylight.

Architect Toshihiro Oki arranged the five
bedrooms to feel like discrete refuges.

Montauk House

Montauk, New York

Desai Chia Architecture

While Montauk is today as recognizable as Quogue or Water Mill, this easternmost village on the South Fork holds on to the laid-back atmosphere that once differentiated it from the Hamptons scene. That persistence may have something to do with architecture. Many local houses feature bedrooms on the first floor and public rooms on the second—an inversion of the traditional house layout that maximizes occupants' access to sunlight and views. The upside-down plan prioritizes interaction with nature over social protocols.

It was Montauk's informality that won over Dallas-based Jonathan and Marianna Yellen as they searched for a beach community where they could construct a place for themselves and their two daughters. Montauk House, completed for the Yellens in 2018 by New York–based Desai Chia Architecture, interprets the inverted layout in a thought-provoking manner.

The building replaces a neglected 1960s-era cottage that had anchored a modest corner lot, the zoning of which prevented Desai Chia from designing more than 2,950 square feet of enclosed space. Studio namesakes Arjun Desai and Katherine Chia explain that the tight fit demanded starting with a rectilinear building, to avoid losing square footage to circulation or dramatic gestures.

Even so, the architects manipulated the volume so that it barely appears boxlike. They inserted a terrace in the north half of the second floor, for example, and removed the southeast corner of the first floor to create a similar outdoor space at ground level. A third terrace lines the south face of the upper story; accessible by an exterior stair and partly enfolded by a cantilevered roof and east-facing wall, the terrace appears carved out of a bigger mass like the two other outdoor elements. Bands of sliding doors on the south elevation and attenuated windows elsewhere echo the appearance of slotting and notching. Desai Chia's layering of exterior materials—burnt-timber board and batten clads the upper half of the house, and the ground floor is made of cast concrete—represents heaviness and lightness in more general terms.

Chia likens Montauk House's play of solids and voids to the use of chiaroscuro in fine arts practice, noting, "When you work with architecture from the perspective of light, you recognize that spatial experiences take place in both form and the absence of form."

Indeed, were it not for its voids, Montauk House might not feel nearly as immersed within the coastal atmosphere as it does. Consider the upstairs: here, Desai Chia diverged from the conventional inverted layout, occupying the floor's north half with the primary bedroom suite and two studies. The slotted terrace on this north-facing side divides Jonathan's and Marianna's studies, yet it is also accessible only from those rooms, providing the parents with an outdoor retreat of their own. In the southern half of the second floor, various living areas meld easily into one another and with the adjacent deck. Proving that this modified plan has had no impact on informality, family members and friends bypass the north-facing formal entry, entering the house via the south terrace's attached stair.

"Usually, architects refer to a contextual design as relating to the angles, materials, or construction methods of a community. Here, the openness of the house, as well as the use of decks and terraces to create flow between inside and outside, creates that sense of place. It's more about a programmatic interest in Montauk than a borrowing of forms, and I would venture to say that the relationship to place is more immediate for it," says Desai. Chia adds that the front yard's extant oak tree, stunted and gnarled by the Atlantic Ocean climate, lends poetry to the indoor-outdoor experience on Montauk House's second floor. As she puts it, "In the Hamptons region, the tree canopy is shaped by weather and soil conditions. Being up in the canopy simultaneously connects you to the power of the coastal environment and frames longer views to the surrounding landscape."

Back inside the house, the ground floor caters to the social lives of teenagers. This interior is meant for the younger Yellens to have some independence, as Desai Chia enlarged the typical entry so that it could be used for hanging out. Bedrooms and a bathroom outline the room on two sides.

Montauk House has several larger, flexible spaces, like the entry-cum-lounge or the office terrace, that allow the house to adapt to a change of plans. When the Yellens commissioned the house, they had imagined using it in summers and transitioning to full-time occupancy once the kids had gone off to college. During the COVID-19 pandemic, however, the family unloaded their Dallas residence and moved into Montauk House for good. Thanks to Desai Chia, the accelerated timeline has not come as a shock. Though the basement has been repurposed in the service of storage and fitness, there have been no reports of crowding or territoriality. Drama isn't really Montauk's modus operandi, after all.

Montauk House is located at the intersection of
two secondary streets not far from the ocean.
Desai Chia Architecture faced the residence's
formal entry away from both routes.

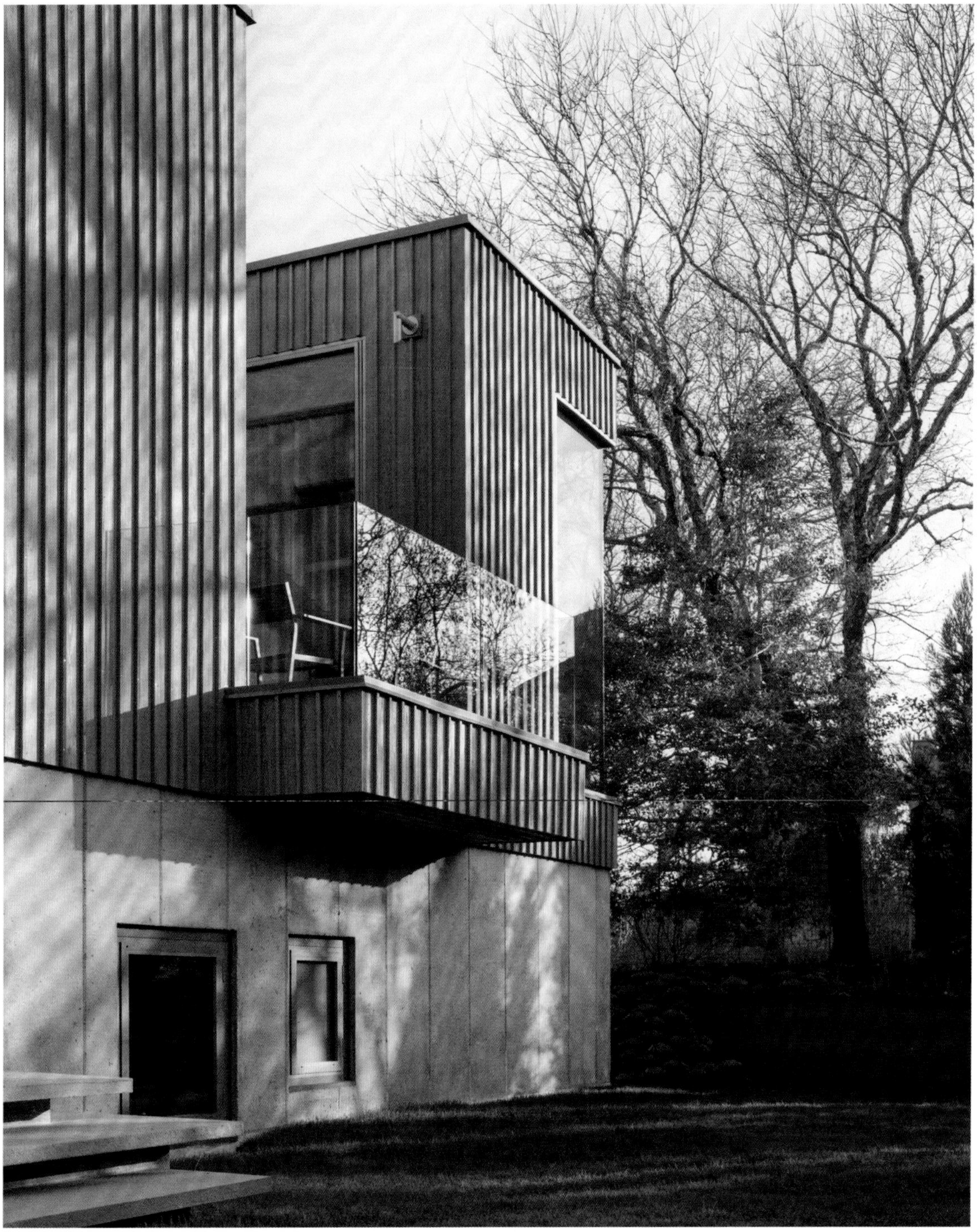

At the second floor, common spaces weave in and out of the building's south elevation—placing family life in neighborly view while maximizing occupants' sight lines to the coast.

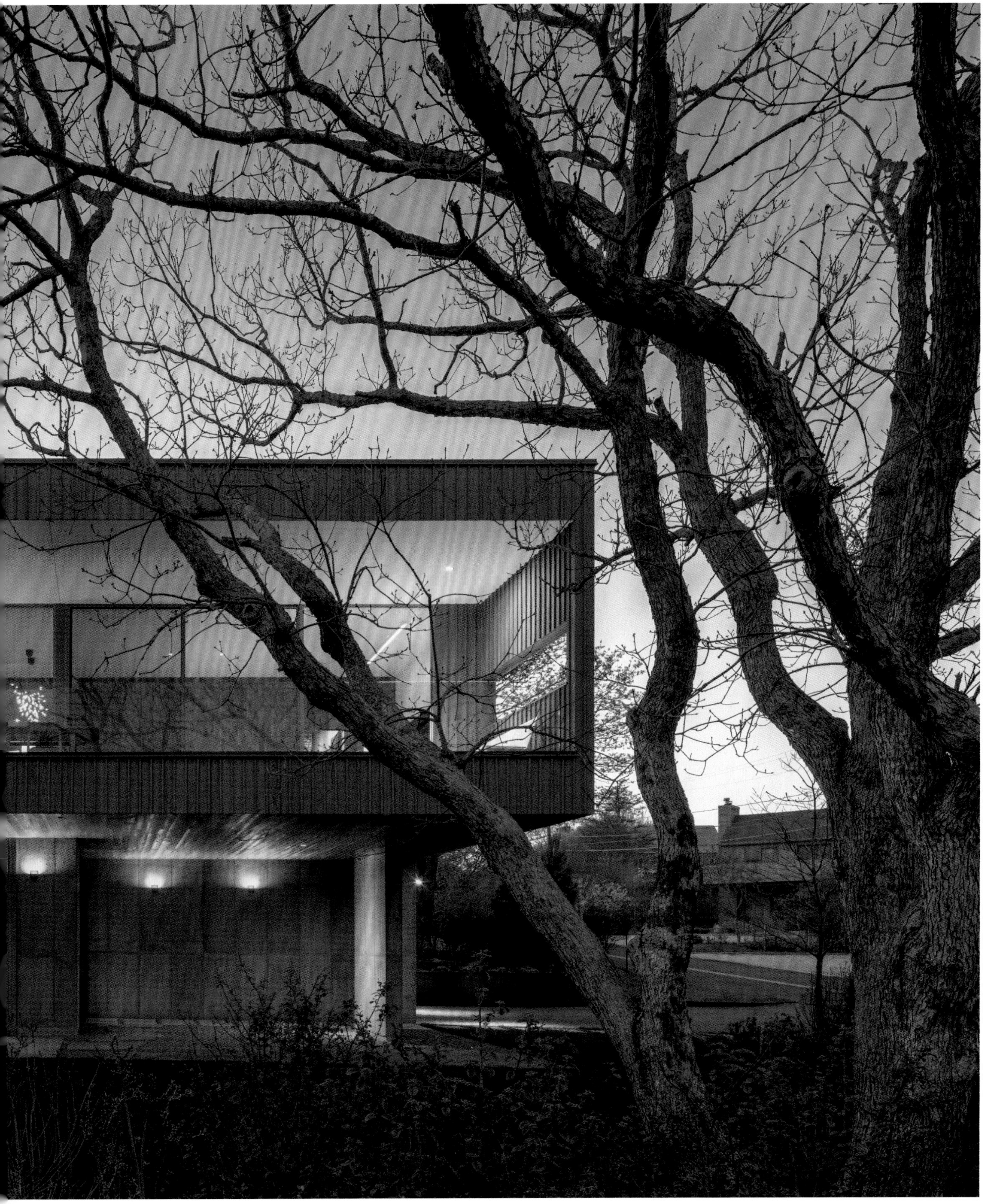

Pike & Pond

Sag Harbor, New York

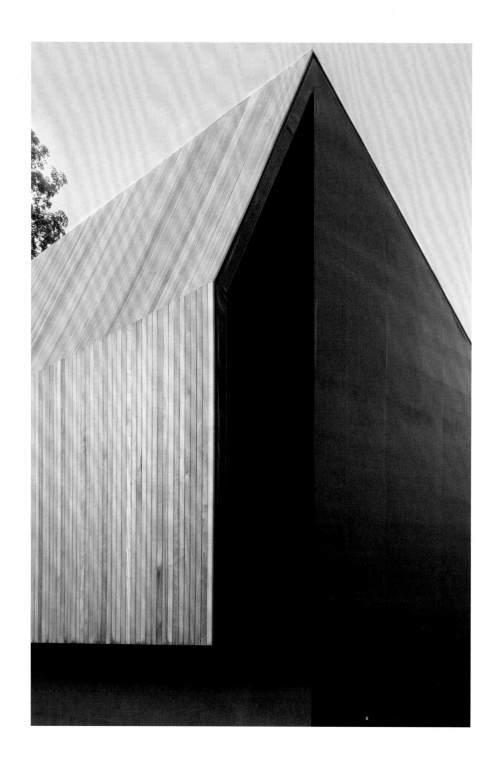

Oza Sabbeth Architects

If you were to read through the interview transcripts behind this book, the term "modern barn" comes up often and pejoratively. Thanks to speculative real estate development throughout the North and South Forks, modern barns have sprung up like so many raised ranches, and architects and homeowners have grown suspicious of their faux sentimentality.

Ask Nilay Oza about the modern barn phenomenon, and the architect will energetically explain why it has taken hold of the East End and how it threatens to dilute more earnest interpretations of the vernacular. Yet Oza, who cofounded Bridgehampton, New York–based Oza Sabbeth Architects with Peter Sabbeth in 2015, is also a realist. Specifically, he notes that local building regulations favor the barn shape. "Across the board, South Fork jurisdictions limit the height of flat-roofed homes to twenty-five feet, whereas pitched roofs can reach thirty-two feet," he says. "That forces you to not presume a classical modernist response to a site, and to instead embrace the pitched roof as a way of providing volume without increasing scale." For his own three-thousand-square-foot home completed in 2018, Oza looked for ways he could harness this regulatory penchant to unique ends.

Known as Pike & Pond, the house is located outside Sag Harbor on a north–south turnpike that connects the former whaling village to the South Fork's main vehicular artery. From the roadway, the half-acre lot descends in a west–southwest direction toward a freshwater pond. In response, Oza placed one gabled volume parallel to the road, and he linked another gable perpendicularly to the house's northern end via a glazed corridor. This transparent element offers passersby one of the only glimpses into the residence, as the west elevation mostly comprises mahogany planks and exposed concrete. Opacity not only lends the project a mystique not otherwise associated with barns as a type, but also veils Oza and his family from passing cars and trucks.

In handling the steep gradient, Oza's scheme turns playful. Rather than level the house to the turnpike, the architect mitigated slope by sinking the ground floor six feet beneath that datum. The house's primary entry is carved into the hill, just in front of the house's west elevation. On the east side of the building, meanwhile, Oza employed expansive windows and basement-level openings to ensure both visual and physical connectivity to the backyard. Retaining walls and terraforming support the overall concept, which effectively allows an occupant to move through and around the house in ways the site would not have permitted without a creative intervention.

That movement reveals additional particularities, such as the southern volume's off-center ridgeline, which hints at the single-loaded corridor within. Continue perambulating and you might wonder about the black exterior membrane not visible from the turnpike. This synthetic rubber is normally layered within a building envelope, but performs just like traditional claddings, so Oza brought it to the forefront. While Pike & Pond's various design strategies would have been thought-provoking in any shape, here they make a case for the pitched roof. In the right hands, even a conventional form can be made surprising again.

Architect Nilay Oza positioned a sunken entry behind a retaining wall at his Sag Harbor home, called Pike & Pond. From the adjacent turnpike, the residence has an enigmatic, floating quality.

Interiors largely frame views to the rear of the half-acre site, which descends to a coastal plain pond.

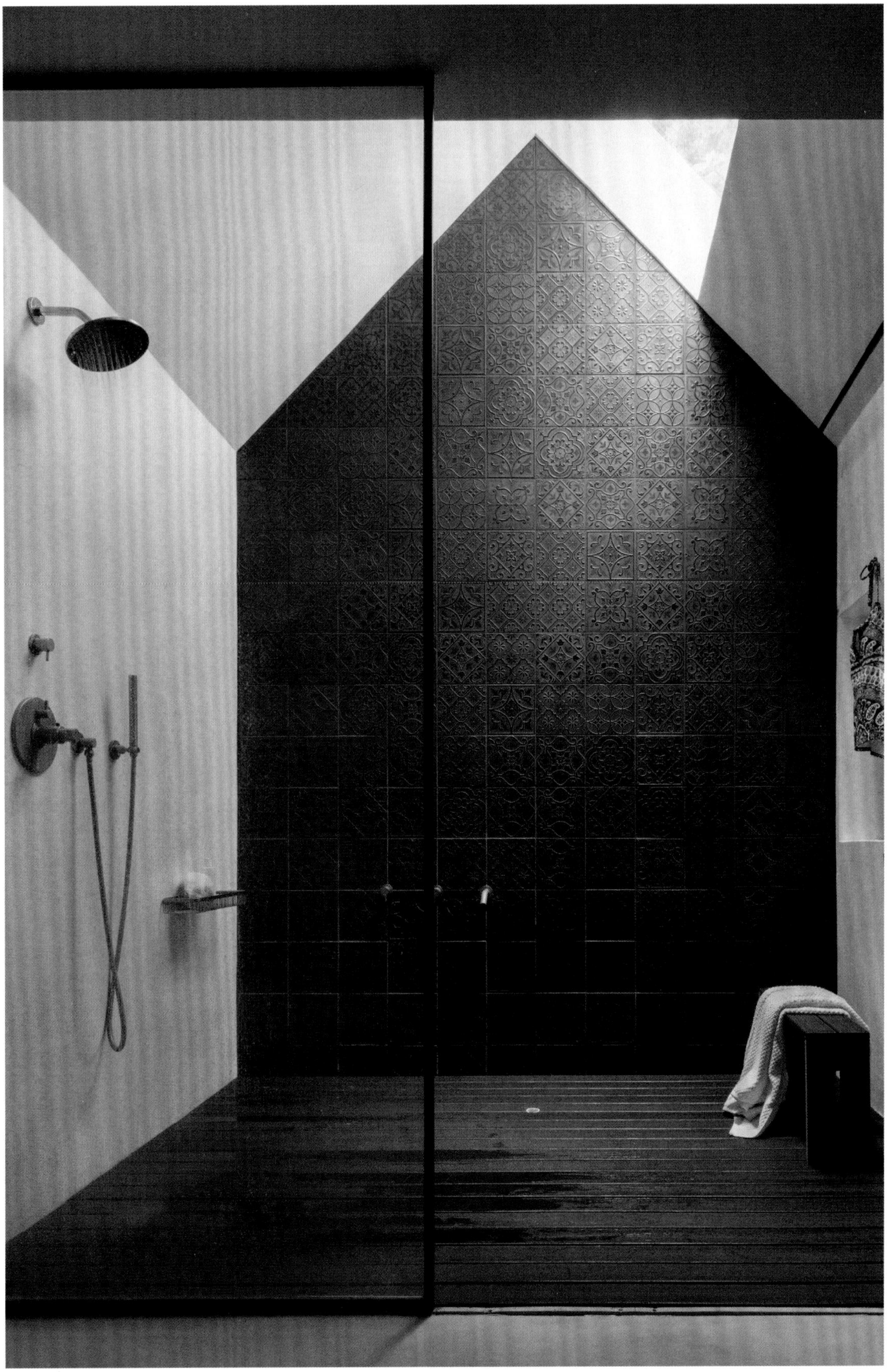

Bar House

East Hampton, New York

Audrey Matlock Architect

Geographically speaking, Long Island's East End is monolithically flat by reputation and wide-ranging in fact. Of course, there are the signature plains running almost to the water's edge, which were formed by the retreat of the Laurentide ice sheet. But this is also a place of hilly forests, angular bluffs, and rolling marshes.

Audrey Matlock experienced the landscape's variability firsthand one autumn afternoon in 2011, when the New York–based architect was combing over the thirteen-acre wooded parcel that Andrea and Josh Reibel had recently purchased in the Northwest Harbor section of East Hampton. "How I start thinking about a building is in terms of its relationship to the context," Matlock says of her search for the best spot for a five-bedroom weekend home for the couple and their two kids. At first glance, the site offered little for inspiration—just swaths of second-growth pine and oak surrounding two unbuildable wetlands. Yet the day's hike revealed a strand of conversation that would become a dialogue. In the south part of the lot near the edge of a five hundred–acre nature preserve, "I realized there was this one area with a twelve-foot change of grade, which was interesting because I saw two faces for the project: the front of the house would engage with an intermediate landscape that bridges the forest and the house, whereas the rear of the house would overlook a garden that is highly manipulated in form." Matlock imagined architecture that could amplify the vertical relief of the slope.

To turn a design concept into a three-dimensional form, Matlock says, "I'm a big fan of bars for houses," referring to long rectilinear volumes. "They're so clean and simple and allow every room to look outside. And there can be more than one of them." Upon completion of multiple study models for Bar House, architect and client gravitated toward a concept comprising two of those elements intersecting at a right angle. The bar that contains front-of-house functions roughly follows an east–west axis and welcomes users in its northwest corner. At its eastern end, there are two guest bedrooms. The remaining bedrooms, as well as a gym and home office, occupy the bar extending to the south. The garden is imprinted in the southwestern crook of this L-shaped layout.

Separating Bar House into public and private realms appealed to the Reibels. Even more compelling was Matlock's treatment of Bar House in elevation: lifting the north–south volume on V-shaped pilotis and placing the only double-height interior at the intersection between bars to enclose the stair that accesses the bedroom wing. The stair's upper landing also incorporates a den, which opens to a terrace and green roof topping the public wing. (The hairpin-like steel frames also form a colonnade along the south elevation of that wing, supporting its grassy crown.) These moves yield some practical gains, such as the ability to tuck an outdoor kitchen beneath the elevated volume, as well as different perches for observing nature.

Indeed, fostering a relationship with the outdoors propelled Matlock through the project's conclusion in 2016. It is no coincidence, for example, that the bar volumes are largely glazed to immerse the interior in views. Nor is it a coincidence that the pilotis echo the multi-trunk birch trees planted in front of Bar House's north elevation. "If you just looked at its parts—a heap of glass and steel and so on—somebody might not believe you would build a house out of this. Yet Audrey understood how much the natural environment would flow through the house," says Josh Reibel. "I have an enormous respect for her discipline."

The architect further explains that she is not conjuring an illusion in which the natural and the manmade are one. "I'm fascinated with incorporating engineering into the aesthetic," Matlock says. "Buildings are about the things that make them." The exterior's steel pilotis are an obvious example of visible engineering. Matlock's interest in a legible human imprint also manifests more subtly, namely in the way Bar House's ten thousand square feet unfold along a four-foot module. Sections of drywall ceiling alternate between four- and eight-foot widths and flat and canted installation. Twelve-foot-wide planes on the inbound side of the north elevation are made to accommodate large-scale contemporary artworks, and these surfaces are interspersed with slots of glass measuring two feet wide. The rear garden's three sixteen-by-twenty-foot plots of shaggy fountain grass, which create a threshold to the pool, even abide that logic. The grid is rigorous, not overbearing, and it speaks to a collective belief in home as a place where one feels safely ensconced in an otherwise disordered world.

"The pandemic gave us the opportunity to spend months here on end, and Andrea and I keep remarking how much more relaxed we feel out here than we do in Brooklyn. The tension goes away, and it's a completely different internal life experience," Reibel concurs. "We want open space that stimulates but does not challenge, and where we can simply be with friends. We're not looking for opulence."

The Audrey Matlock–designed Bar House abuts a
nature preserve that, measuring 515 acres, was
the first large parcel that East Hampton had ever
acquired for the purpose of open space protection.

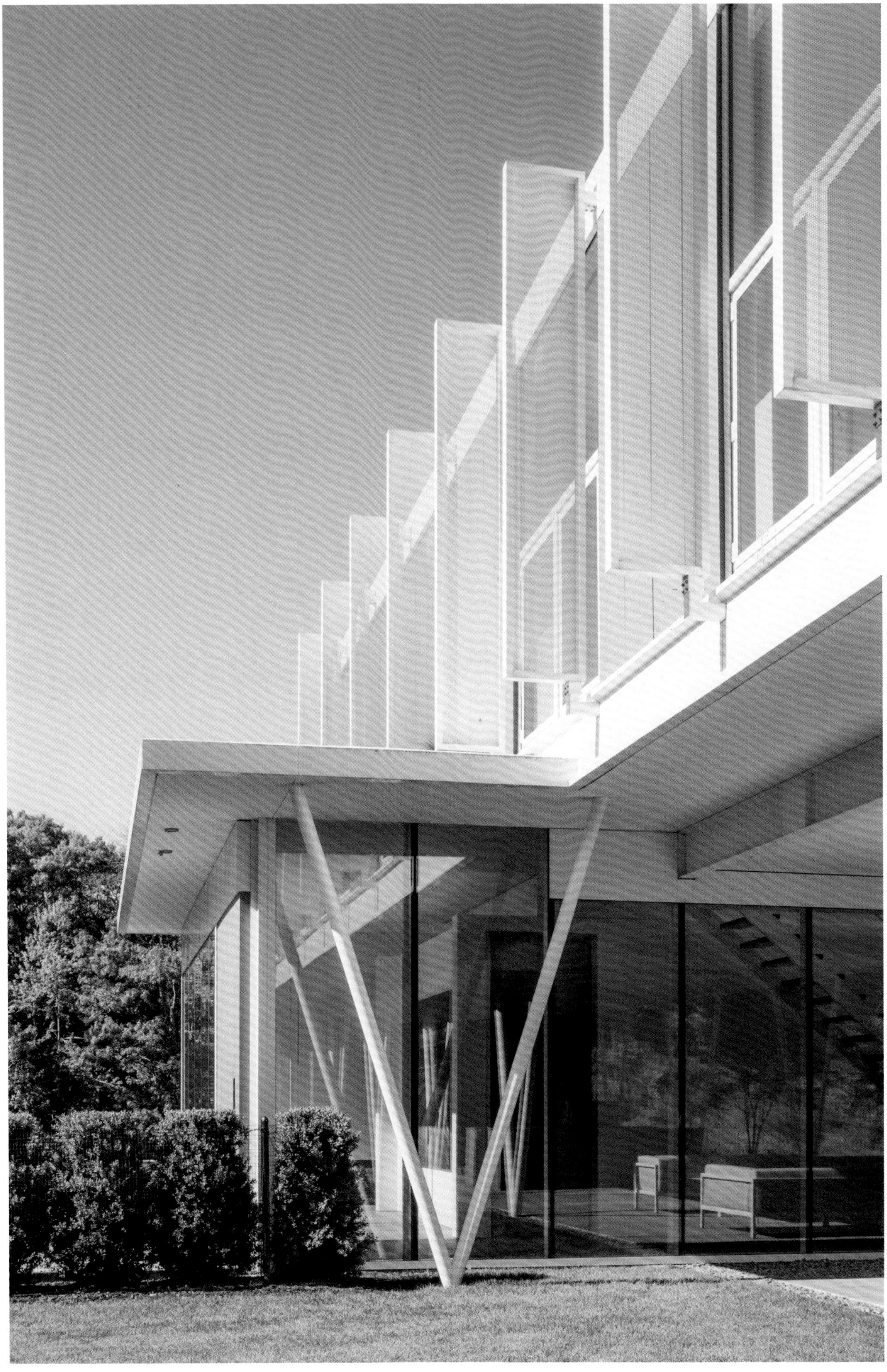

Over the course of their relationship with Matlock, homeowners Andrea and Josh Reibel have become avid collectors of art. In turn, along the north elevation of Bar House, the architect placed panels of zinc that correspond to display surfaces inside.

Shore House

North Haven, New York

Leroy Street Studio

Before New York–based Leroy Street Studio earned the commission to design and build the residence known as Shore House, its homeowner had spent five years waiting for the North Haven property to come to market. He spent another five years scrutinizing the west-facing 1.8-acre site, where the trees thin out as the topography rolls into Noyack Bay—as though it had been intended for watching sunsets.

The decade of interrogation was galvanizing for architect Marc Turkel, who cofounded Leroy Street with Morgan Hare in 1995. "Sometimes, you have the chance to work with someone who brings an enormous amount of energy and inspiration to a project," Turkel says of the client, whose brief advocated for the site's natural qualities. "He wanted a place to listen to the rainfall, hear the waves, and experience the transition from woods to the expansive view. Our understanding of the project and of the landscape would not have evolved so quickly without all of his accumulated knowledge."

Because the client had felt a sense of discovery in the transition from copse to coastline, Leroy Street amplified that experience with Shore House. The architects tucked the easternmost side of the building's meandering, 2,600-square-foot ground floor into the hillside and balanced a bar volume atop its western portion. The newly arriving visitor observes only the slim, blackened cedar-clad bar before descending to the threshold. As one journeys past the entry, rooms transition from partly subterranean to fully exposed. Glimpses of Noyack Bay become views and panoramas, and the boundary between indoors and out generally dissolves.

While the success of the design hinged on the client's wisdom about the site, Turkel notes that design-build delivery tailored the house even more to the pleasures of nature. Often, building a custom residence can be a process of handoffs, in which disciplines weigh in one at a time. To put it in overly simple terms: architect conveys designs to engineer, who relays construction drawings to contractor, who then hands the house keys to the interior designer. Yet for Shore House, Leroy Street's architecture, interiors, and construction divisions all took part in the entire process. That integration revealed opportunities for improvement that might have been overlooked or undercommunicated otherwise.

"We were putting up one of the entry walls, which we had designed around a particular artwork," Turkel says by way of an example. "When we visited the site, the [structural] framing pointed out an incredible water view, so we changed that surface to a portal. It would have been impossible to grasp that opportunity without interacting with construction in real time." The architect credits design-build for optimizing several other vistas and for incorporating reclaimed materials into the interiors. He also foresees Leroy Street engaging in this highly collaborative method for as many as half of its future commissions.

"To unlock the most intriguing aspects of a building, there is no substitute for time," Turkel says. "By getting involved with interiors, with construction, we can extend our time with a project to yield a whole different level of results."

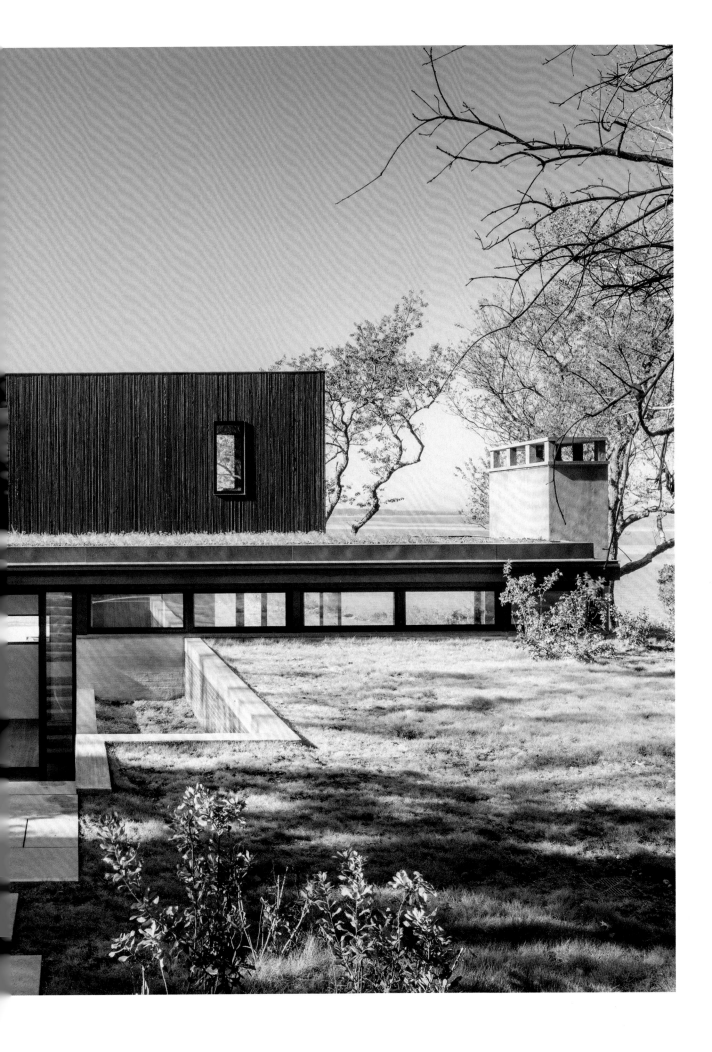

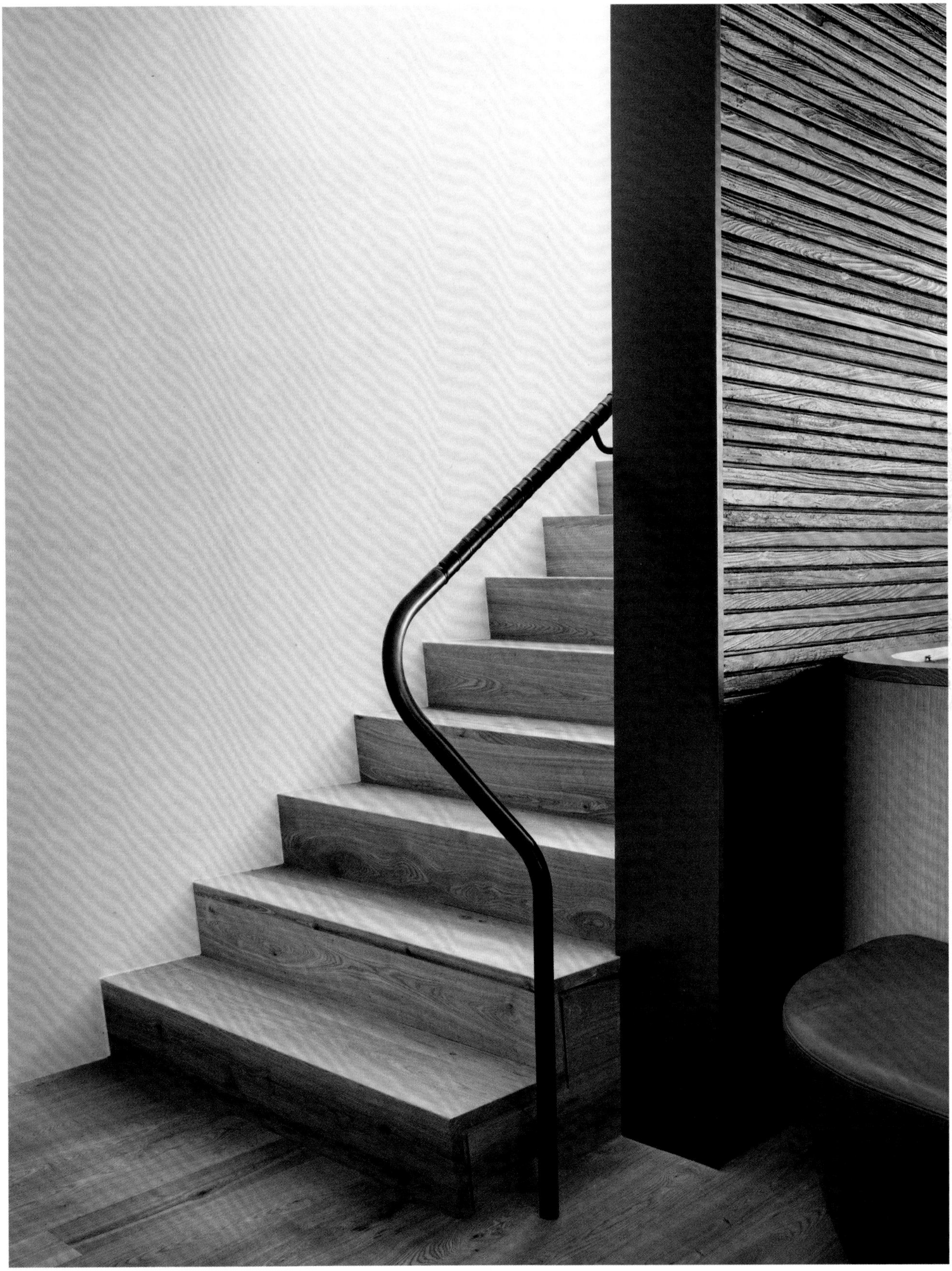

The experience of Shore House is one of
anticipation and discovery. Leroy Street Studio's
multidisciplinary project team composed
the residence as a procession of screens and
frames that reveals increasingly unfettered
views of Noyack Bay as one moves into ever
more private rooms.

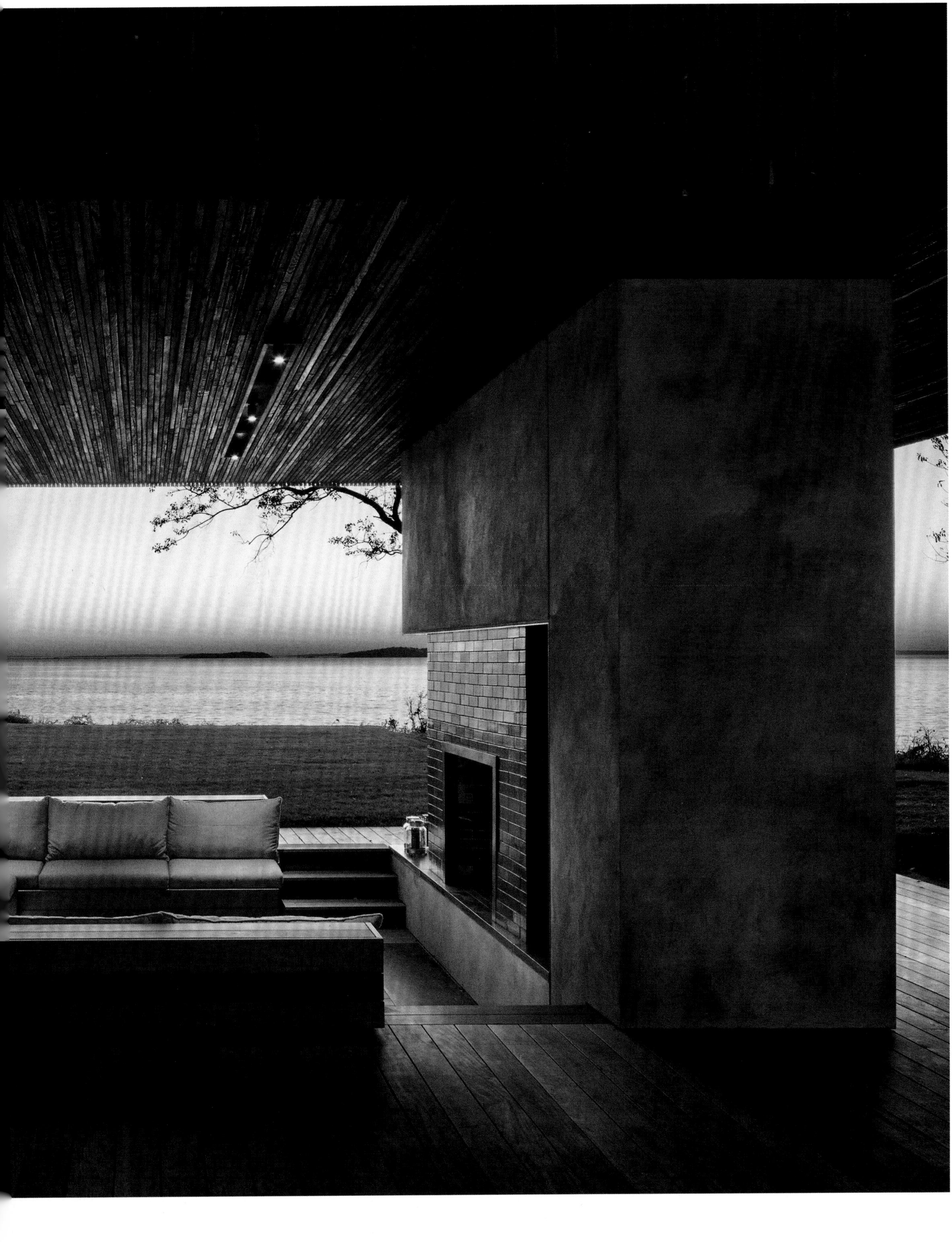

Shelter Island House

Shelter Island Heights, New York

Christoff:Finio Architecture

In 2014, Martin Finio and Taryn Christoff were several weeks into crafting a summer home for Taylor Antrim and Liz Twitchell on Shelter Island and were feeling stumped. The cofounders of Christoff:Finio Architecture had already determined that middling water views didn't necessitate a tall solution. They also planned to distribute the house's functions among three pavilions, allowing for the house to appear more proportionate to its 2.7-acre site. But where should the pavilions be placed, exactly? And what precise shape should the trio take? The following morning, Finio headed from Christoff:Finio's Manhattan office to Shelter Island, to pace the site in the remaining daylight.

By dusk, Finio realized why he kept returning to the flag lot's eastern edge. Even though this zone backed up to houses facing the street, it maximized the vista of Antrim and Twitchell's own property as well as views of conservation land to the north and west. "Being close to the neighbors without facing them directly let me enjoy the expanse of land without looking into the sun," Finio recalls of the visit. As the design process unfolded, the house would trace this eastern boundary along a north–south axis.

Back at the studio, the architects reconciled this new realization with practical knowledge, namely that it's more affordable to electrify and plumb a single building rather than a compound. The result of their design iterations—completed in 2017—unites the three-part program via a continuous roofline and floor plane. Assuming an irregular boomerang-shaped footprint, public rooms are flanked by a group of three bedrooms and a guest suite to the north and south, respectively. "We wanted the parts to seem like they had been dropped there," Christoff says of the plan. A wedge-like volume pulls the central volume upward to enclose a studio that glimpses the Shelter Island coastline.

By covering the mostly low-slung volumes in one stroke, Christoff:Finio's scheme also encompasses three decks, a glassed-in walkway placed between the living area and bedrooms, and a courtyard immediately west of that walkway. These connective spaces lend a more commanding presence to a house that just tops 2,800 square feet, and Finio notes that they embody a kind of "productive ambiguity, where an exterior might be enclosed or an interior might be open. We like the idea of softer boundaries where people play out their daily rituals."

The house's western elevation leans into the liminal. Window walls alternating with semi-enclosed deck spaces invite Antrim, Twitchell, and their two kids to look upon, brush past, or interact with the meadows and woods however they desire. As for the east elevation, those nearer-than-expected neighbors behold a sculptural cedar form. "We wanted the public face to be muted, in terms of conveying some idea of what's going on behind it," Finio explains of the largely opaque facade. He adds that there's something about Shelter Island that welcomes the unconventional gesture, saying, "Although the ferry ride lasts only a few minutes, in that time you feel yourself shedding the social pressures of your everyday life; being floated over to this community is uniquely liberating."

Approaching it from the property's long driveway, first impressions of Shelter Island House lean toward the monolithic. The Christoff:Finio design is in fact porous: structure and landscape interchange with ease.

Homeowners Taylor Antrim and Liz Twitchell reside largely on one level, except for a small upper-story volume that is accessed from the living area.

Christoff:FInio sited Shelter Island House toward
the edge of its 2.7-acre parcel to make the
landscape feel larger and untamed.

Setting New Precedents

Q&A with Margot and Clay Coffey

There's a thread that runs through these pages. From preservation to innovation, the people and architecture featured in *Hamptons Modern* are fixated on the local—on saving, divining, and reinterpreting the character of far-out Long Island. This book's third and final section, "Setting New Precedents," proposes benchmarks against which future place-makers might measure their success.

Wealth inequality, climate change, unthinking densification—thanks to qualities as diverse as its status-conveying reputation and flat coastal landscape, the East End is a crucible of the phenomena with which citizens everywhere are grappling. But the East End is also host to efforts to mitigate these trends, and even to imagine a more just and sustainable community. That residents and design teams are integrating such vision into single-family homes feels like a natural extension of the region's architectural heritage; where experimental architecture during the twentieth century largely hinged on technological advancements, it now investigates long-term-minded performance.

For highly local solutions to global challenges, keep an eye on architect Clay Coffey and writer and designer Margot Coffey. Margot is a native Long Islander, and she and Clay launched Isaac-Rae Studio on Shelter Island in 2012. The husband-and-wife team then relocated the multidisciplinary venture to Brooklyn and more recently moved it again to Greenport, New York, picking up acclaim for intriguing form-making and youthful resourcefulness along the way. In this interview, the Isaac-Rae cofounders reflect on the love of place that propelled them to the North Fork, as well as the role of emerging architecture in keeping the East End lovable.

Margot, looking back on your Long Island upbringing, would you say you feel a calling to the East End?

MC My relationship with the North Fork started early. My family came out to East Marion every summer starting in 1985, and later we moved out there for good. I have distinct memories of elegant old beach houses sitting next to stilted houses, simple shacks, and reclusive cottages. The only thing they had in common was an easygoing and wind-worn shabbiness. A bit of effortlessness. This also gives you a sense of the people. There has always been a quiet enclave of people that comes here to hide, create, or rest. Then there are the year-round locals, who take pride in the more rural lifestyle. In both sets, there is simplicity and goodness—working with your hands and nature and getting back to life's essential qualities. I think there's room for a new North Fork aesthetic that can keep this in mind. We've been working on house prototypes that interpret modernism for a deeply rooted, modest place. We're avoiding the "modern barn" vernacular and instead looking at new geometry, materiality, and formats that are ripe for adaptation.

The North Fork has long been the least convenient, least inhabited place on Long Island. I love its out-of-the-way nature, and I love the people who are keeping the relationship with the land and sea intact. Many of our friends are farmers, winemakers, fishermen, and other people who work thoughtfully with the natural elements of this place. I see art and artists as a major part of this group, even if the connection to nature seems less overt. There's a level of small-scale development that can really help this community thrive.

You mentioned a house-prototyping exercise in passing. May we expand upon that—namely, do you think you could accomplish an agenda like this more emphatically or quickly, if you were aiming it toward the South Fork?

CC When we look at "award-winning" or critically acclaimed residential architecture, you're right that the majority of that work is being done on the South Fork.

MC It's also true that there's more work, capital, people, and demand for modern architecture on the South Fork, and we'll almost always be engaged with that market as a result. But I wouldn't discount the interesting or unexpected work that arises on the North Fork.

Is there a commission that was essential to Isaac-Rae's formation?

MC Clay's work on Andrew Geller's Green House was one that inspired us both and brought our ideas closer together. The unexpected nature of Geller's work made an imprint on me, and, in the end, the fun he was having disarmed me. Fast-forward to our Blue Marlin project: it originated from a seemingly standard renovation of a dilapidated house with an uninhibited view of Shelter Island and the Peconic Bay—a very North Fork opportunity—and we saw one great yet unlikely way to revive it. I believe in the idea that living in less conventional spaces, built with beautiful proportions and an awareness of the surroundings, can shape how you live in the world.

Margot and Clay Coffey pictured in their Greenport workspace, a former Masonic Temple that they share with the beloved antiques purveyor Beall & Bell.

Prior to opening your studio in Greenport in 2021, Isaac-Rae was based in several locations. Do you find that running a North Fork–based practice is different from working in New York, or does it feel like an extension of the city?

MC If anything, the North Fork continues to be the outlier. People here are curious and engaged, but they tend to hold on to the region lightly and invest in it cautiously. In some ways, as a North Forker, I share our local pride in this sentiment. The area is not glamorous; it's not here to impress you. In other ways, it's frustrating that we haven't made more strides in building a progressive community with more diversity and more opportunity for a middle class of artists, farmers, and small business owners, which I think would make it a more sound and successful market.

CC Working on the East End is in almost every way different from working in the city. The market, while affluent, is small and residential—it is almost entirely driven by clients who have second homes. There is also very little commercial or cultural work here, although we have some ideas.

I sense that you've given a lot of thought to zoning, is that right?

MC No community needs another soulless shopping center, especially on Long Island. I feel that any new commercial projects on the North Fork should have purpose and show awareness of local character, sustainability, and natural surroundings. I'm also pretty concerned about uninspired commercial renovations. There are a few very large commercial buildings on the North Fork that will likely need a new purpose soon.

CC Zoning laws are always an issue. I think zoning laws could be relaxed in certain areas but not in all. It's a hard line to walk, as you don't want irresponsible or unconsidered development—but you also want to be pro-growth and to develop towns and villages in ways that help the actual people who live in the community. We champion zoning laws that support small-scale commercial development that benefits local farmers, craftsmen, and creators. Zoning that promotes that kind of social and cultural development is not currently a reality on the North Fork.

Has Isaac-Rae's mission for the built environment changed since you committed to living and working on Long Island?

CC I'd like to build formally novel, environmentally positive work. We have always wanted to approach each project first from an unconventional and artful perspective and then layer in the unique design limitations and opportunities that arise. I was trained in a Louis Kahn–based education that focused heavily on art and design. Margot is a writer and experiential designer who has worked with institutions on a spectrum of conceptual designs. Our common ground has been atmosphere—the essence of a place. Practically speaking, this has translated into working with unexpected geometry and divine proportions in each project.

MC Something that has always been a part of our process, but which has come to the forefront in recent years, is this awareness of place. We've been interested in the project site from a holistic perspective. What are we starting with that we want to carry through? Outside the city, we can take subtle cues from nature—it can be as simple as a small grove of trees you want to preserve or a spot to create privacy where there is none. Working with the water, wind, and sun is a true touchstone. What's best about this approach is that it begins with a respect for nature, and from there so much can be sustainably driven.

Isaac-Rae projects include the restoration and expansion of an Amagansett house that architect Andrew Geller had completed in 1968, as well as a forthcoming, dramatic transformation of a Southold house known as Blue Marlin.

Are there certain nascent trends that might unlock the next wave of expression, whether by yourselves or another studio?

MC COVID-19 has transformed a portion of the market, especially on the North Fork. We've seen that a lot of people are renting in the city and buying out here. New, environmentally sound requirements that have been coming into effect over several years are a good thing. Clients aren't resisting this. We've had several clients come to us with interest in passive houses, which we think is great. At the same time, region-wide building codes are tending to get more and more restrictive, and this could create further issues or new workarounds in the market.

Springs House

Springs, New York

Michael Haverland Architect

The East Hampton, New York, residence that architect Michael Haverland occupied until last year has been a point of reference for East End homeowners since the building's completion in 2004. Designed for himself and his partner, Philip Galanes, this home is a rare instance of timeless modernism. Fans often remarked on the house's evocation of Maison de Verre by Pierre Chareau, whose only stateside commission had stood in East Hampton. While Haverland was indeed inspired by the Frenchman's affinity for sweeps of gridded glass, he spaced the muntins and mullions at his home to recall Shingle Style architecture. By candidly revealing the house's structure, he also paid homage to the writings of Robert Venturi and Denise Scott Brown, for whom he had worked prior to opening his own practice. In all, the architect synthesized wide-ranging concepts and motifs into something that is both enduring and unique to the Hamptons.

Thanks to his home's instant-icon status, Haverland transformed from relative newcomer into local institution practically overnight. But the architect has handled his notoriety delicately by avoiding cut-and-paste assignments that might otherwise stymie creative growth.

Haverland's story of incremental yet continual change is nicely encapsulated by the Springs House project, a commission that also illustrates how his academic process has as much appeal as his design output. Research for the project again crisscrossed generations of amassed wisdom. This time Haverland paid closer attention to nearby modern houses whose sites resembled the wedge-shaped two-and-a-half acres at hand. He also made sure to incorporate Frank Lloyd Wright's Usonian houses into the historical journey, because the client had expressed fascination with that component of the legendary architect's work.

"Every site is different, and every client is different, so it doesn't suit site or client to replicate a previous solution—nor to appoint something to a project that doesn't come from analysis and understanding," Haverland says of his studious methods. "Just philosophically speaking, I don't believe reusing schemes is an appropriate way to approach architecture. Then there's the Hamptons' legacy of inventiveness, and the kind of moral imperative I feel to be part of that continuum."

In response to the parcel's southern orientation and coastal topography, Haverland distributed Springs House's five thousand square feet into an intersecting pair of fourteen-foot-tall rectilinear volumes that, in plan, form a reversed L whose stem points north. Taking a cue from local modernist precedent, Haverland conceived windowless north elevations to guarantee the homeowners' privacy from passing vehicles. Meanwhile, walls of steel-framed glass, which hark back to Haverland and Galanes's own residence, largely greet the other cardinal points. The south elevation is placed behind a colonnade to shade the interior, buffer the glass from coastal storms, and enhance the threshold between house and pool; the rhythm of stucco-clad columns breaks to accommodate an outdoor dining vignette.

To conceal the north faces of Springs House, Haverland skewed toward inventiveness. Digital fabrication was just beginning to emerge in this mid-aughts period, and Haverland proposed using the technology to create the building's shroud. He generated a twenty-by-twenty-inch foam mold comprising vertical and horizontal undulations, from which the client cast 970 concrete blocks by hand. The blocks were then fastened to the building's curtain wall in an alternating pattern that Haverland likens to an abstract plaid. The rippled surface shucks rain without staining, while nodding ever so slightly to the exterior masonry of Wright's Usonian houses. Haverland explained his aim: "I was trying to find an architectural vocabulary that had all the attributes of modernism without making any overt historical citations."

Since wrapping up Springs House in 2009, Haverland says he "[tries] to push the envelope on several aspects of every project." He recently got to do just that with Springs House itself, when new homeowners invited him back for an update that was completed in early 2020. At first glance, Haverland's job was to oversee a handful of adaptations that better suited the family of four, such as making a bathroom more kid-friendly and coaxing daylight into the media room that's tucked into the building plinth. The architect accompanied that work with improvements upon his original scheme, weaving cast-concrete block into the interior entry and relandscaping the hillock that contains the plinth.

In response to the new client's desire for a freestanding workspace, Haverland also explored the cutting edge. Limited to 150 square feet due to wetland restrictions, the architect inscribed two lines into the earth. One line, thick and straight, is clad in the lead-coated copper that more traditionally-minded Hamptonites might associate with roof drains; the other forms a gentle sine curve finished in vertical planks of teak that—like the cedar shingles that are so common on the South Fork—gray with the passage of seasons. He sited the pavilion among a stand of white oaks off the southwest corner of the main residence and rotated it approximately forty-five degrees from the house's axis to face sunsets more directly.

Between the pavilion's two solid planes, Haverland devised a wedge-shaped volume that rakes upward as it moves from northeast to southwest.

All three sides of this insertion are single sheets of structural tempered glass, testing the limits of the material. "We wanted the form to be something that both contrasted with the house and related to the softness of the landscape, but which was still modern," Haverland explains. He further calls the pavilion "a piece of jewelry for the house," although it is equally appropriate to think of this brooch as one in a series of gambits that are guiding a career and a region.

Planes of hand-cast bricks conceal Springs House's most visible elevations from passing vehicles. Approaching the residence's public threshold on foot, the concrete surfaces part to reveal a glass-and-steel envelope.

Architect Michael Haverland rewards entrants to Springs House with soaring interior volumes and poignant connections to daylight, weather, and Accabonac Harbor.

Amagansett Modular

Amagansett, New York

mb_architecture

After architect Maziar Behrooz finished renovating a home for an artist friend in Amagansett, New York, in 2007, the client requested using the remaining budget to design a freestanding studio. Behrooz had become fluent in Quonset huts as an inexpensive alternative to framed construction, yet a prefabricated semicircular building didn't suit this brief. Where would the homeowner hang her artwork, after all? Instead, Behrooz carted two $2,500 shipping containers to the site; by placing the containers atop a traditional foundation and partly peeling away their undersides, he completed a small, ground-floor workspace that opens to a double-height atelier at the basement level. The project—completed in 2009—came to a total cost of only $95,000.

This project and its price tag went viral. Staffers at mb_architecture, which today operates offices in New York and Sag Harbor, fielded nonstop inquiries about shipping-container homes on the East End and farther afield. "At the time, many of my friends were beginning to be unable to afford living or building in the area," Behrooz recalls. Feeling a call to service, he pivoted from Quonset huts to shipping containers as a solution for housing more people, more affordably. "You shouldn't have to be a millionaire to afford a house."

Behrooz's journey has since followed two tracks. One has been dedicated to testing the creative limits of shipping containers at roughly three hundred dollars per square foot, which is the nationwide average cost of new construction (but one-third of the average per-square-foot cost on eastern Long Island). The Amagansett Modular house pictured here represents the culmination of those efforts thus far.

Conceived for Amy Fusselman, Frank Snider, and their three children, Amagansett Modular centers on a quartet of shipping containers stacked into a two-story rectilinear volume. Behrooz tethered a half-container to the core's south elevation to contain a primary bedroom. To the north, a breezeway connects the core to one additional container that serves as a bedroom wing. The core and wing are staggered in the site plan, so the breezeway may skirt a mature oak tree. This composition also focuses attention to the west, where the house's base steps down to a landscaped pool area ensconced in second-growth woods.

Behrooz reflects that the path toward Amagansett Modular has been remarkably fulfilling. "These projects feel like a continuation of design experiments by Andrew Geller, Charles Gwathmey, and Barbara and Julian Neski, which lured me to the East End to begin with," he says. But the architect also notes that affordability nags at him still. The only way to beat the three-hundred-dollar figure is to minimize both design customization and on-site finishing work. In response, Behrooz has pursued that second track, conceiving a collection of one-story residences that homeowners can shop much like they would an automaker's models and trim options. While COVID-19-related supply-chain problems have made it difficult to estimate an average construction cost for this new initiative, Behrooz feels confident of its greater affordability. Design commissions employing these shipping containers are already underway.

Amagansett Modular "fits into the landscape harmoniously, yet is anything but a shrinking violet," says homeowner Amy Fusselman. Of architect Maziar Behrooz, she adds, "A lot of Maziar's houses seem to fit naturally where they're placed but don't cower."

Enormously wide stairs are a recurring feature of Behrooz's shipping-container homes. The architect says that that breadth not only makes the entire interior appear larger, but also lends the space an amphitheater- or even temple-like quality. "We've had only positive responses to our home and I'm certain it's made other people think differently about the potential of shipping containers," homeowner Frank Snider notes.

Wetlands House

Orient, New York

Ryall Sheridan Architects

Located on the easternmost tip of the North Fork and separated from mainland Long Island by a mile-long causeway, Orient, New York, is an end-of-the-world place. It also feels like a step back in time, thanks to the working farms and waterways—rather than suburban-style development—encircling its antique downtown. Clifford and Leslie Cohen made an important contribution to this protective band of open space in 2013, when they acquired four-teen-and-a-half acres of marsh and former potato fields and asked New York–based Ryall Sheridan Architects to conceive a home that celebrates the site. The result, known as Wetlands House, is as civic-minded as it is pleasurable.

The Cohens have been members of the Orient community since 2005, when they purchased a circa-1850 sailor's residence in the hamlet's historic center. The husband and wife had frequently biked past the site of Wetlands House and—intrigued by its persistent emptiness—finally phoned a local realtor to learn more about the property. Leslie remembers the inquiry being anything but serious, yet "two weeks later, the realtor called back to say, 'I found the owners and they're willing to sell.' We thought this was crazy. We thought we might spend six months in Rome rather than build a house." Attraction to the property—as well as a sense of obligation to defend it from subdividers—scuttled the Rome plan and led them to contact architect Bill Ryall.

The client was imagining a single-story residence thoroughly ensconced in the landscape. Considering the destruction wrought by Hurricane Sandy when it glanced Long Island in 2012, however, Ryall presented a disarming hypothetical to the Cohens: how would this building fare if the next hurricane were to hit the North Fork directly? Ryall suggested lifting the house ten feet above ground to evade storm surges and tidal anomalies, events bound to take place even in the absence of climate change.

Dispensing a twelve-foot ladder to the site, Ryall then invited the Cohens to try on his proposition for size. Their climb revealed painterly southeastern vistas of the Peconic River and Gardiner's Bay. And from the bird's-eye view, the foreground appeared more like tapestry than vegetation. They fully committed to Ryall's outlook. "It was not our original thinking, but we were excited by that one move's ability to resolve so many criteria," Cliff says. "Right away we knew we wanted this view," Leslie notes, "and we wanted it to be the heart of the house."

Ryall Sheridan started its design from this heart, in turn. The team placed a linear volume atop totemic concrete walls to enclose public spaces. In plan, this volume resembles a single quotation mark facing southeast; in elevation, it combines cedar cladding, floor-to-ceiling windows, and a screened porch. To the west, a two-story bar parallels the southern half of the first volume and contains the primary suite upstairs and two bedrooms below. Restructuring of the site allows the pair of guest rooms to access the outdoors, as the Cohens had initially envisioned.

An east–west connector encompasses stairways and intermediary rooms, including the entry and a perch-like study, while mediating the change of grade. A raked roofline frankly reflects these functions, and an exterior path that reaches southward allows users to regard the roofline's angular expression as well as the relationship between built and natural environments. Rather than embed a building within the landscape, Ryall Sheridan "allowed the landscape [to] run through the house," as recently minted partner Niall Carroll puts it. The scheme revels in nature while remaining mindful of its power.

Cliff remarks that the process of siting and massing Wetlands House was highly participatory as well as "painstaking." Throughout the dialogue, architect and client "spent a lot of time thinking about how we would affect people—how they could enjoy the scene as they always had, with minimal interruption from the house. The essence of this statement is that our sense of stewardship has only grown as we got deeper into the design."

This stewardship manifested in the steps that followed. "If you think the land is important, then it's easy to add an environmental agenda," Ryall adds. The Cohens commissioned New York artist and environmental activist Lillian Ball to remove the invasive vetches and mile-a-minute weeds that had been choking out indigenous shrubs and grasses. Simultaneously, Ryall Sheridan applied its expertise in passive-house sustainability to the project, sourcing triple-glazed windows and adding a rubberized membrane to the building envelope to better insulate the interior, among other techniques.

Completed at the turn of 2017, the results are environmentally high-performing and personally memorable. A super-efficient building envelope is slightly thicker than the norm, for example: Ryall Sheridan leveraged that fact by placing the sills of the water-facing windows and sliding doors beneath the finished floor. The edge disappears and the effect is one of floating. Outside, the horticulturist and aesthete alike will delight in the passage of seasons, as asters' starburst-like blooms steal the spotlight from swaying goldenrod, both making their way for the vermillion fruits of chokeberry bushes to glint in the winter sun. Leslie recalls a recent conversation as particularly emblematic: "A friend of ours who lives down the road said there had been a lot of talk about our house. I told him I hoped we hadn't stolen the view from anyone. And he said, 'Are you kidding? Your house is the view.'"

Visitors approach the formal entrance of
Wetlands House from the northwest (opposite);
the residence seen from its walkway, which juts
to the southwest (above).

While Ryall Sheridan Architects' design of Wetlands House is a combination of comforting enclosures and spaces blurring interior and exterior, coastal daylight and bay and wetlands views are always within easy reach.

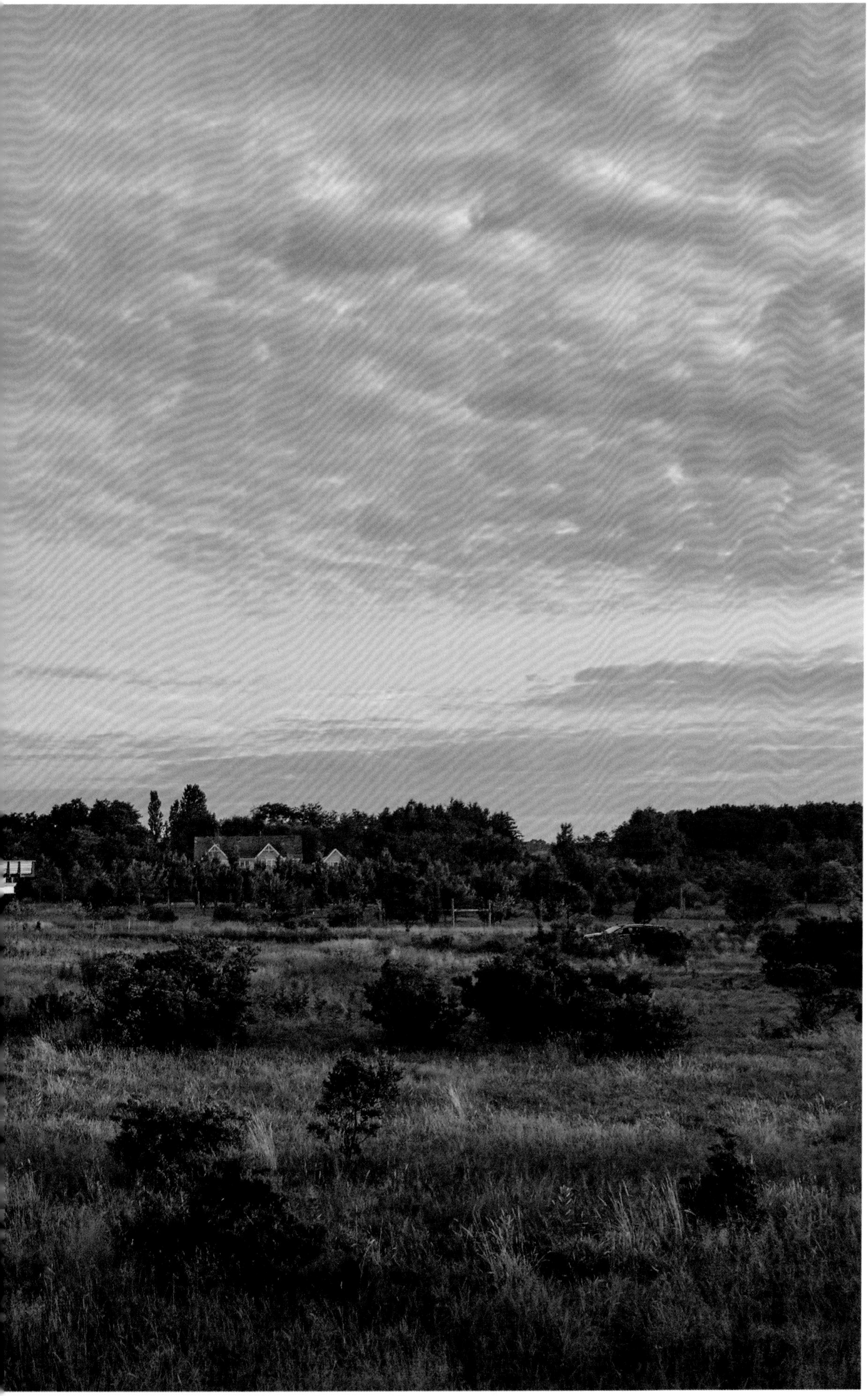

Cocoon House

Southampton, New York

nea studio

The Southampton carriage house that has been in architect Nina Edwards Anker's family for the past five decades exemplified, when it was completed in 1890, how a structure could blend into its natural surroundings. Designed by Stanford White in the period's prevailing Shingle Style, the structure evoked the colors and irregular forms of the landscape. The guest cottage known as Cocoon House—which Anker completed in the rear of the 3.6-acre site for herself, her husband Peder Anker, and their two sons in 2019—represents a significantly deeper relationship with the earth. The founder of nea studio approached nature not as a visual muse but as a partner in building performance and occupant well-being.

After Anker earned her master's degree in 2001, she and Peder were based primarily in Norway, and the couple spent their stateside visits in the White-designed carriage house as guests of Nina's brother Philip. After Nina and Peder had their first child, the vacation headquarters shifted from Philip's domain to an existing seven-hundred-square-foot rear cottage that Nina made more livable by retrofitting it with a fireplace and sliding doors. "Everyone was so relieved when this got built," Anker recalls of the accessory's upgrade. "That's also when I fell in love with making tiny places that look big."

By 2010, the couple began to consider demolishing the 1950s-era cottage (which didn't conform to Southampton wetlands protections) and creating room enough for the still-growing family. "If you're going to take on a time-consuming project, you really want the process to keep you curious," Nina recalls, feeling underwhelmed by her initial drawings of a modern barn. Yet the architect, who was studying for her PhD in Oslo at the time, had just taken a course in passive solar design that struck a chord. "Passive is basically the idea of opposites: the north half of a building is opaque and protected from the elements, while the other half is crystallized to collect thermal mass from the south," Anker says. When she sketched this section on to an L-shaped plan that abided by Southampton's setback rules, she knew she was on to something.

The single-story, 1,438-square-foot design "really took on a life of its own after I got fascinated by this idea of a round screen that expresses the movements of the sun." To the generously insulated north and west elevations, Anker applied an apostrophe-like curve that reaches a maximum interior height of sixteen feet. The geometry offers several practical benefits, such as expediting interior air circulation and reducing sonic reverberation. It also has a symbolic value beyond embodying solar pathways, namely paying homage to Shinnecock wigwams, about which Anker says, "I believe we lose something when we incorporate avant-garde, global technologies without also embracing cultural memory or sense of community." The architect specified an all-wood structure for its low embodied carbon and lack of asthmagens, and she finished those north- and west-facing surfaces in cedar shingles, because she "didn't want to stand out like a sore thumb."

Cocoon House's south and east elevations are assembled entirely of sliding glass doors. Together they form the inbound faces of the L and measure sixty-five feet in total. This elbow abuts a cistern-fed reflecting pool; besides storing rainwater for irrigation, the pool experiences evaporation whose cooling effect catches southerly and westerly ocean breezes and drifts through the house. In wintertime, low-angle sunshine penetrates closed doors to warm the interior. Heating derived from the electric grid supports Cocoon House during the coldest months, while sixteen photovoltaic panels, mounted to a nearby garage rooftop, power the residence in its entirety for the sunnier majority of the year.

Exemplifying Anker's original idea of a crystalline volume, angled skylights top all the sliders. Raking toward the billowing, cedar-clad roof, this glass surface oversees Cocoon House's main circulation route. The corridor that traces the east elevation accesses the home's sleeping quarters and here, the skylights are tinted in a north–south progression of colors from yellow to red. Anker explains that the palette is a reference to Goethe's argument that yellow and red could respectively stimulate alertness and slumber, adding that new research about circadian rhythms confirms the German writer's theory.

Anker believes that Cocoon House further proves the relationship between the physical environment and human perception. In addition to prompting senses by recreating the midday and setting sun via the tinted skylights, Anker placed the pool immediately next to the house in part because water has a calming influence, and she says that the project's overarching connectedness to nature eased her family's permanent move back to America. She adds that Cocoon House's combination of energy efficiency and active sustainable technologies is a natural consequence of effect serving affect, as she terms it: "When you become aware that a house is powered by sun, wind, and rain, your awareness of our planet's resources is also awakened."

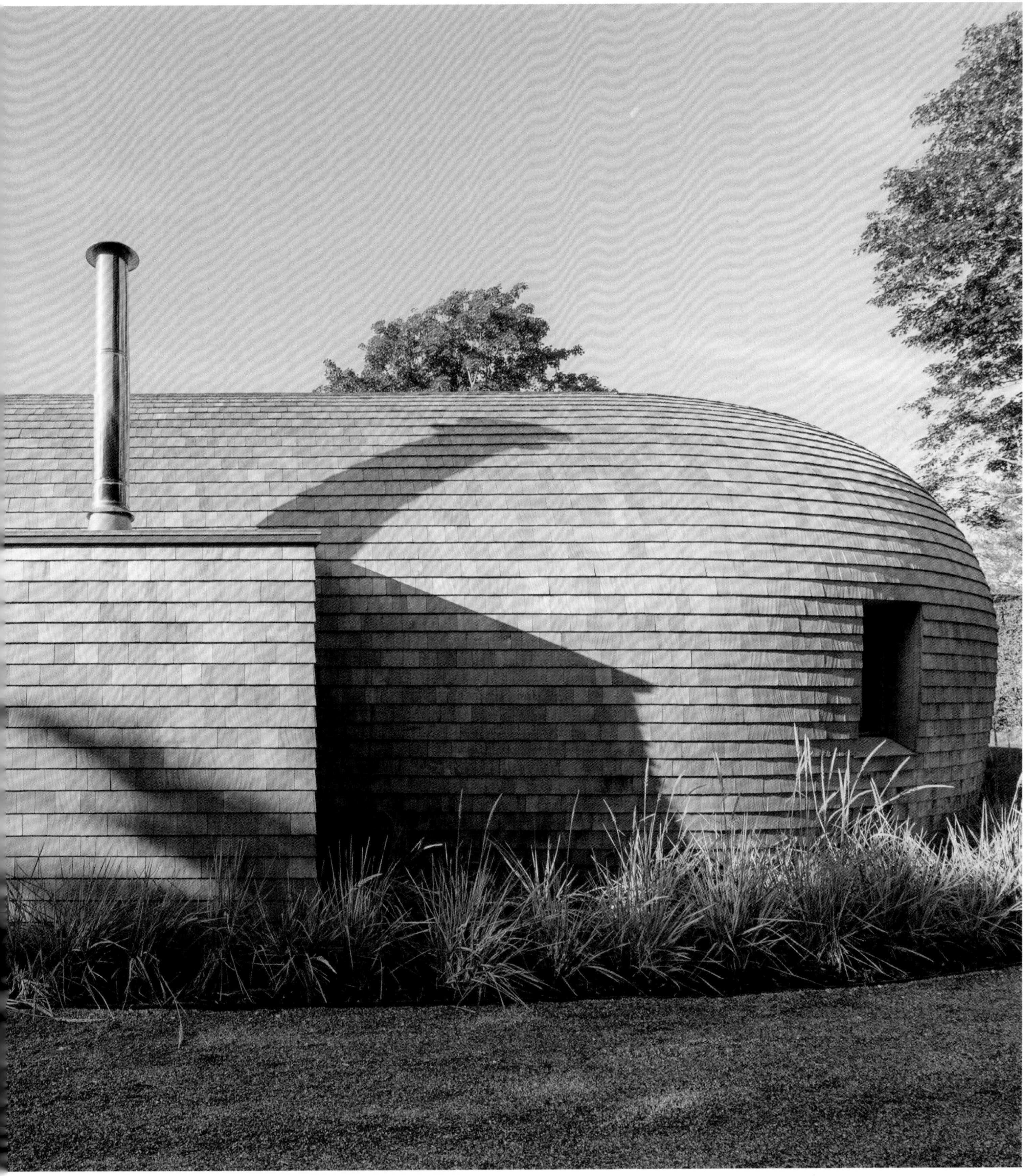

Nina Edwards Anker lined the crook of Cocoon House in a rainwater-fed reflecting pool, which provides a passive cooling effect for the house on warm days when sliders are open. Water has a calming effect on the psyche, as well.

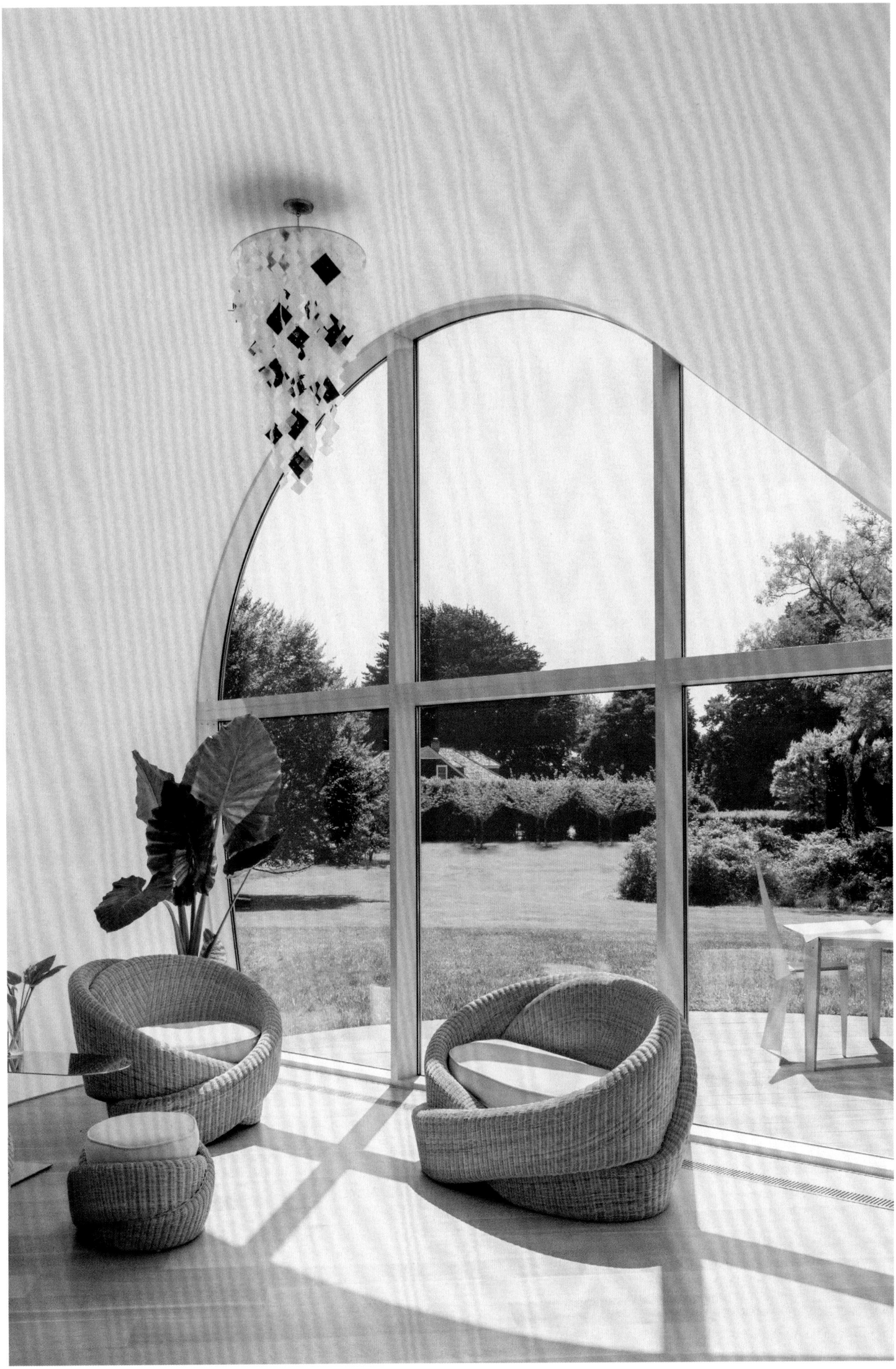

Anker considered her family home at every scale—from landscape and built form down to living- and dining-area chandeliers that the architect had made by interlacing photovoltaics and seashell.

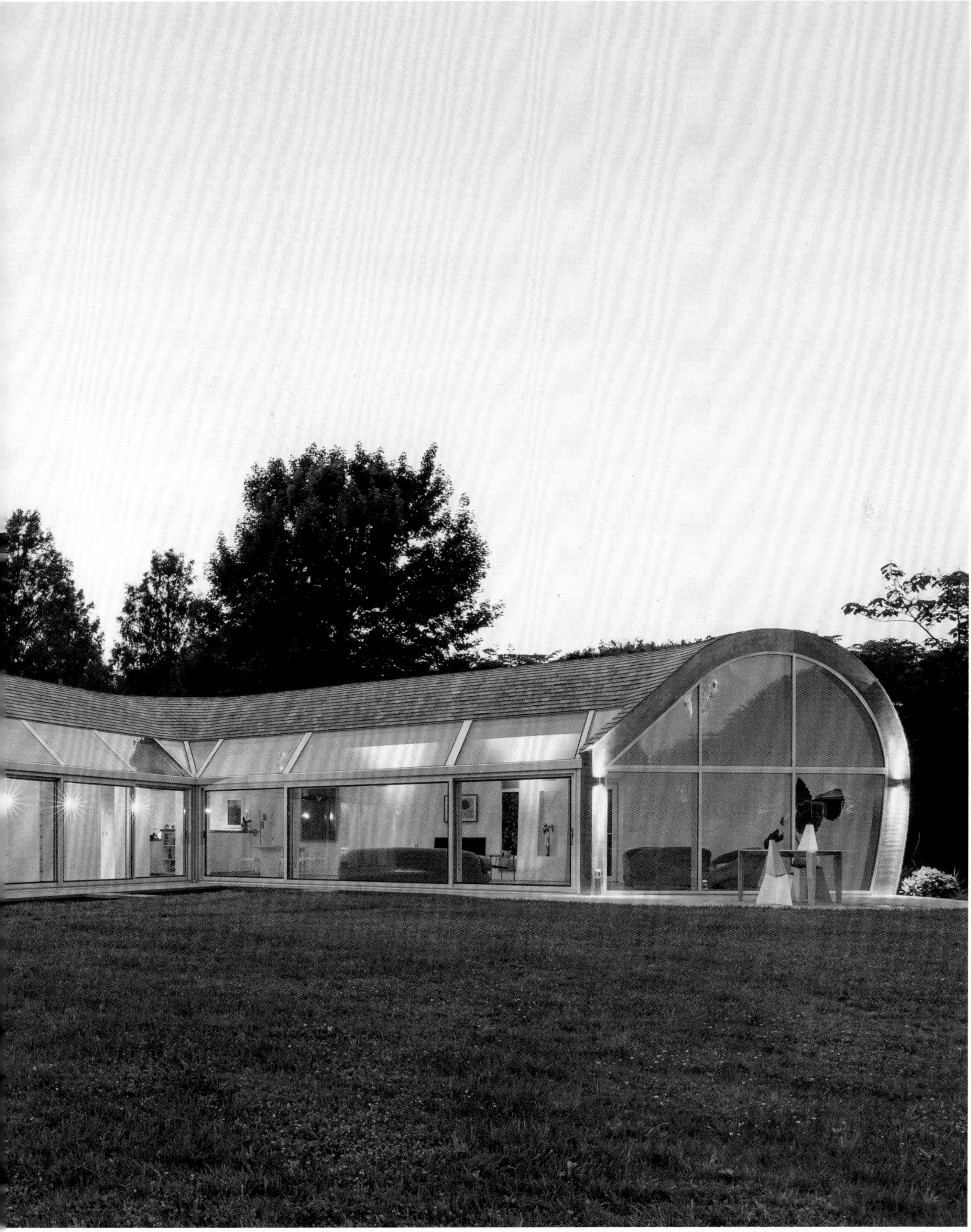

Elizabeth II

Amagansett, New York

Bates Masi + Architects

According to the criteria by which the architecture community traditionally judges a residence, the home that Paul Masi created for his wife Elizabeth and their three children genuinely deserves the multiple awards it has received since 2014. Located on a half-acre flag lot just south of downtown Amagansett, New York, the building is a striking yet meditative antidote to the hamlet's historic fabric and bustle. Distributing 3,200 square feet into a constellation of spaces that surround a south-facing ground-floor deck, the house balances a need for belonging with one for alone time, while reflecting the family's shared love of the outdoors. Interior functions are legible to the casual onlooker. An east–west long axis represents best practice for solar exposure. The layering of differently sized planes and volumes deftly mediates between landscape and structure.

But the house is arguably more remarkable for what can't be seen—or heard. Masi, of the highly regarded East Hampton–based Bates Masi + Architects, explains that acoustical privacy was the foremost driver of his scheme. Masi had completed a family home in the area once before, in a remote location that demanded automobility. Wanting their kids to move freely between school and activities, Paul and Liz arduously combed listings for a building site over several years. When they finally identified this property, "The first thing that came to our minds was noise," he says of the seasonal crowds and ceaseless traffic nearby. "That planted the seed of the design."

These circumstances also launched Bates Masi into a wide-ranging education about acoustical engineering, which guided the shape of the house. Consider the northern elevation, in which a series of landscape and structural walls illustrates the layering effect most overtly. These planes direct one's attention to the primary entry as they emerge from and dissolve into the landscape; in fact, they also function as buffers shielding occupants from the din of Amagansett's commercial center. The shortest, freestanding walls form the first layer of noise protection, while the tallest wall rises from the foundation to enclose the second floor's single-loaded bedroom corridor.

Acoustics also determined how those walls were constructed. To prevent sound transmission, Bates Masi detailed a twenty-inch-thick wall of poured concrete surrounded by insulating foam. Their outermost surfaces largely comprise foot-wide cedar planks held in place by stainless-steel clips,

which the design team prototyped more than fifteen times to ensure a snug fit. The overall assembly underlines those qualities that are more traditionally lauded, such as durability and energy efficiency. Installing cedar planks via fasteners allows the wood to naturally expand and contract, and the walls' concrete cores provide significant thermal mass that reduces heating and air-conditioning demands. They pay visual dividends, too. "The clips provide a delicate contrast to the massive walls," Masi says. "They enhance one another."

Inside the ground-floor public space, the clips behave as hinges, and the planks pivot in and out to reveal noise-absorbing felt sandwiched between the insulating foam and cedar. The wood reverberates sound when it lies flat on the wall, whereas the underlying felt dampens noise when the planks hinge outward. As a result, the walls may be open and shut until the desired acoustical environment is achieved.

"When I started the project, I may have had a false preconception that we would have uniform acoustical perfection," Masi says of the tunable interior walls. "But I learned that acoustical standards depend on the activity taking place. Sometimes a space should reverberate more brightly—perhaps you're entertaining, and you want to amplify the energy in the room—and other times you want to effect more intimacy. It's exciting to have moved from an expectation of singular acoustical performance to this idea of accommodating a range of experience." He adds that, while an occupant can tune the walls on an event-by-event basis, the cedar planks remain consistently flush during the warm weather, when the interior is open to the deck. The felt is more visible in winter, when acoustically reflective, south-facing, floor-to-ceiling glass is folded back into place.

Experiencing the many benefits of Bates Masi's research firsthand, the firm's namesake is now incorporating those lessons in its wider body of work. The clips have been redesigned for greater manufacturing efficiency, and select residential commissions feature adaptations of the acoustical strategies employed in Amagansett. Masi says that, like any singular approach, form shouldn't necessarily follow acoustics universally. Yet, as the East End densifies and homeowners increasingly prioritize walkable neighborhoods, noise mitigation may become as important as the aesthetic and performance standards that currently define excellence.

A noise-blocking assemblage of planes
surrounding the Elizabeth II entry blurs the
boundary between built and natural environment
and lends a momentous feeling to the act of
threshold crossing.

The interiors of Paul and Elizabeth Masi's Amagansett home boast a restrained finish palette of oak and cedar, as well as stainless and weathering steel.

Monacelli greenlit *Hamptons Modern* in 2018, on the eve of the publication of *Hudson Modern.* But to a son of Long Island, this book required a lifetime of observations. I dedicate it to my parents Carol and Steve, who encouraged me to craft observations with precision and to transform descriptions into uniquely personal commentary. I also dedicate this project to Rick East—my partner in 2018 and now my husband. Rick, thank you for carrying our little family through a challenging project in this most challenging time in recent memory. You have done it with grace, humor, and vulnerability. I can only imagine how you will further blossom when the clouds part.

I have had the good fortune to see Rick's depth of character reflected in all the folks who supported this storytelling. The pandemic could have depleted your attention or enthusiasm in *Hamptons Modern.* Instead, Sophie Benedetti, Josie Cerbone, Gong Chen, Paula Dragosh, Chris Grimley, Eva Hagberg, Jedd Hakimi, Melissa LeBoeuf, Alana Leland, Noah Marciniak, Candace Opper, Danielle Rago, Joey Rake-Delaney, Alan Rapp, Kyle Rottet, Honora Shea, Ted Sheridan, Vicky Ting, Michael Vagnetti, and Bailee Weatherall embraced the requests, nudges, flubs, and brainstorms that attended my work. Alongside the architects, photographers, and homeowners named in this book's pages, your efforts made this survey the comprehensive and evocative document that it is.

Thank you for reading *Hamptons Modern.* It was your interest in its predecessor book that made this project possible, and your continued enthusiasm should likely bring about several more *Moderns* to come. In the meantime, please consider other ways to express your interest in this special corner of the world. AIA Peconic, Group for the East End, Hamptons 20 Century Modern, Hamptons Community Outreach, Heart of the Hamptons, LGBT Network, LongHouse Reserve, Onna House, Oysterponds Historical Society, Peconic Land Trust, Preservation Long Island, SAGE Long Island, Sag Harbor Community Housing Trust, and the Southampton African American Museum are just a few organizations that are worthy of your curiosity and support.

Library of Congress Control Number: 2022938437

ISBN 978-1-58093-594-4

10 9 8 7 6 5 4 3 2 1

Printed in China

Design by Chris Grimley and Josie Cerbone, OverUnder

Monacelli
A Phaidon Company
65 Bleecker Street
New York, New York 10012

www.monacellipress.com